MOON

52 THINGS TO DO IN
AUSTIN
& SAN ANTONIO

CHRISTINA GARCIA

CONTENTS

Hill Country and Beyond

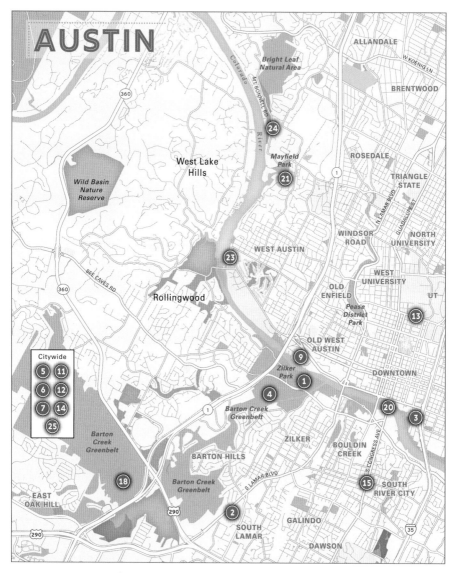

AUSTIN

ALLANDALE

W. KOENIG LN

BRENTWOOD

Bright Leaf
Natural Area

ROSEDALE

Colorado River

360

MT. BONNELL RD.

24

Mayfield
Park

West Lake
Hills

TRIANGLE
STATE

21

Wild Basin
Nature
Reserve

WINDSOR
ROAD

NORTH
UNIVERSITY

N. LAMAR BLVD

GUADALUPE ST

23

WEST AUSTIN

WEST
UNIVERSITY

BEE CAVES RD.

OLD
ENFIELD

UT

360

Rollingwood

Pease
District
Park

13

OLD WEST
AUSTIN

Citywide

5   11

6   12

7   14

25

9

Zilker
Park

1

DOWNTOWN

4

20

3

1

Barton Creek
Greenbelt

S. CONGRESS AVE.

Barton
Creek
Greenbelt

ZILKER

BOULDIN
CREEK

BARTON HILLS

18

15

SOUTH
RIVER CITY

Barton Creek
Greenbelt

S. LAMAR BLVD.

EAST
OAK HILL

290

2

GALINDO

35

290

SOUTH
LAMAR

DAWSON

6

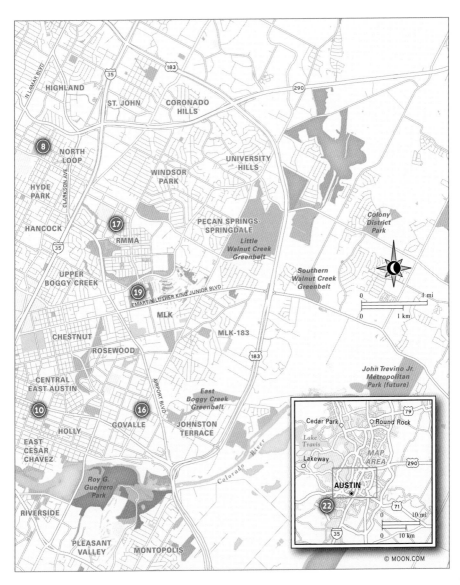

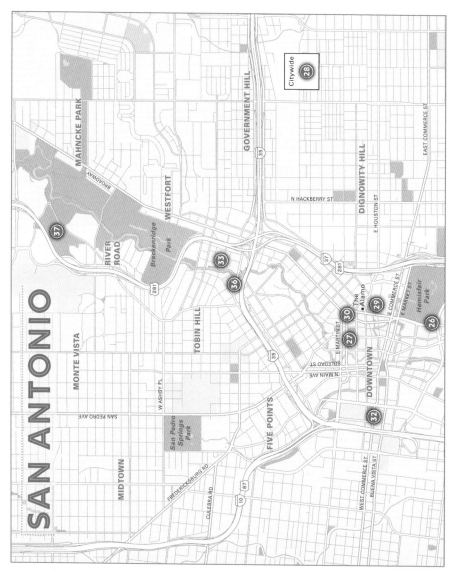

SAN ANTONIO

MAHNCKE PARK

WESTFORT

RIVER ROAD

Brackenridge Park

BROADWAY

GOVERNMENT HILL

DIGNOWITY HILL

Citywide (28)

EAST COMMERCE ST

N HACKBERRY ST

E HOUSTON ST

(37)

(33)

(36)

(37)
(281)
(35)

The Alamo

E COMMERCE ST
E COMMERCE ST

E MARKET ST

Hemisfair Park

(30)
(29)
(26)

MONTE VISTA

TOBIN HILL

E MARTIN ST

(27)

N MAIN AVE

SOLEDAD ST

DOWNTOWN

SAN PEDRO AVE

W ASHBY PL

San Pedro Springs Park

FIVE POINTS

(35)

(32)

MIDTOWN

FREDERICKSBURG RD

CULEBRA RD

(10)
(87)

WEST COMMERCE ST

BUENA VISTA ST

8

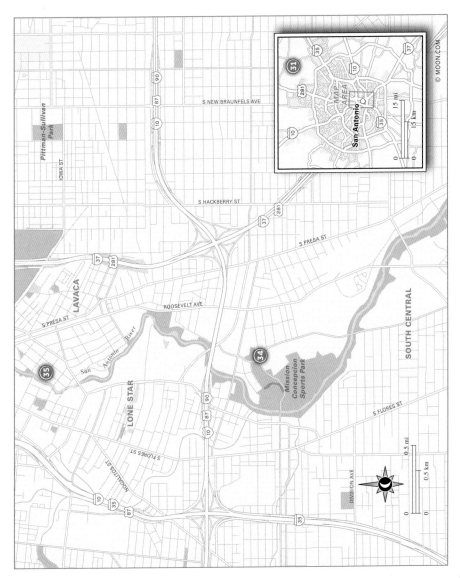

HILL COUNTRY
AND BEYOND

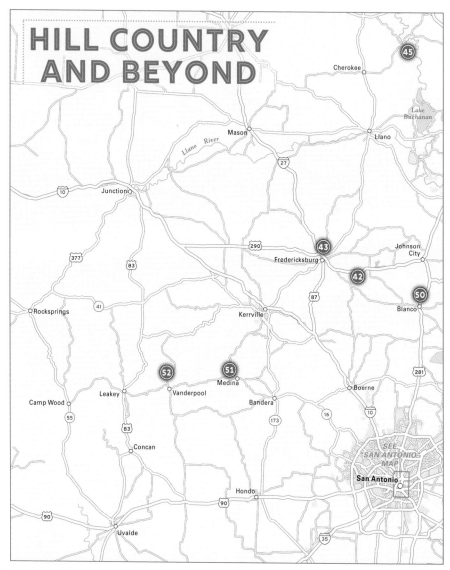

Cherokee

Lake Buchanan

Mason

Llano River

Llano

27

10 Junction

290

Fredericksburg 43

Johnson City

377

83

42

87

50

Blanco

41

Rocksprings

Kerrville

281

52

51

Camp Wood

Leakey Vanderpool

Medina

Boerne

55

Bandera

16

10

83

173

SEE SAN ANTONIO MAP

Concan

San Antonio

90

Hondo

90

Uvalde

90

35

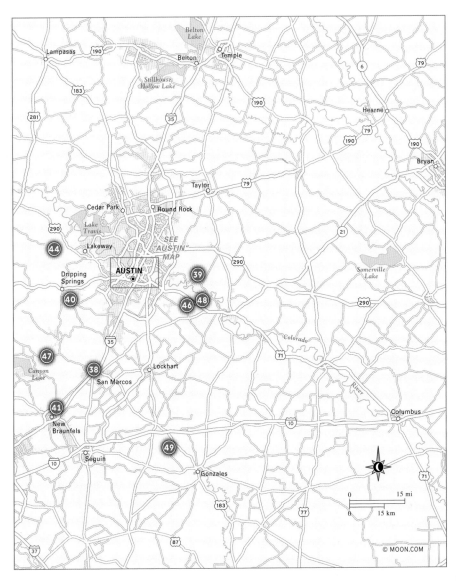

THIS IS MY AUSTIN

What will it be that makes you fall in love with Austin? Its artistic soul? Its incomparable dining and drinking? What will really send you head over heels is its laid-back, relax-and-stay-a-while attitude. This is a city where you can go out in pajamas and feel right at home.

Our food scene is world class yet unpretentious. We're as proud of our food trucks as we are of our James Beard award winners. Butcher paper is piled high with tender brisket, hot pierogis from the farmers market melt in your mouth, and our hippie heritage means the vegetarian options are showstoppers. Care to sip something strong? How does a wine or whiskey trail sound? What about a distillery reviving an ancient desert spirit?

The stars at night are, of course, big and bright, so our nightlife buzzes with energy. You're guaranteed laughs at comedy shows, snacks at drive-ins, and exquisite cocktails along Rainey Street. In the dancehalls, we do the Lord's work teaching beginners how to two-step to twangy songs about heartbreak. Never forget this is the live music capital of the world, where upstarts play alongside superstars.

You can't talk about Austin without talking about festivals. In addition to famed South by Southwest and Austin City Limits, there are events nearly every week that capture the city's fun-loving atmosphere, overflowing talent, and all-around joy.

With over 300 days of sunshine each year, it's no surprise we love a chance to bliss out in nature. Go waterfall hunting, urban kayaking, or jungle hiking. The rolling Hill Country unfolds in a kaleidoscope of colors if you catch it at the right time, with roads like gentle roller coasters offering sweeping views.

San Antonio beckons from the south, with a uniquely preserved lens on Texas *en español*. Rich Mexican traditions are everywhere, from refreshing *paletas* and mouthwatering tacos to the annual Fiesta. See this sister city from a bike along the Mission Trail or from behind your fingers on a ghost tour.

This proud piece of Texas packs in the flavor and the fun. It's amazing bites, a stiff drink on a night out, a local band catching fire, and a day in the sun. Try it all. Savor all the weirdness that makes Austin, Austin. And don't forget your sunglasses.

kayaking in Austin

TO DO LISTS

Hike & Bike

6 Save a horse, ride a **bicycle**

18 Hike the **Greenbelt**

31 Explore underground at **Natural Bridge Caverns**

34 Bike the **Mission Trail**

43 Get away to **Fredericksburg**

45 Find every waterfall at **Colorado Bend State Park**

49 Explore a Texas jungle at **Palmetto State Park**

52 Hike through fall colors at **Lost Maples**

Get on the Water

1 Howl at the moon in **Zilker Park**

9 **Kayak** beautiful Lady Bird Lake

18 Hike the **Greenbelt**

38 **Float the river** in San Marcos

44 Take a dip in **Hamilton Pool**

45 Find every waterfall at **Colorado Bend State Park**

Sip Something Strong

3 Go bar-hopping along **Rainey Street**

12 Sip a **craft brew**

40 Drink ancient **desert spirits**

42 Sip your way through **Texas Wine Country**

47 Drink with the devil at the **Devil's Backbone Tavern**

50 Sip liquid sunshine on the **Texas Whiskey Trail**

Taste of Texas

⑤ Taste Texas at addictive **barbecue** joints

⑭ Eat like royalty at **food trucks**

⑰ Eat your way through the **best farmers market** in Austin

㉖ Unwrap an ice-cold *paleta*

㉘ Eat **tacos** for all three meals

Nightlife

2 Learn how to **two-step** at a hoedown

3 Go bar-hopping along **Rainey Street**

7 Laugh your heart out at a **comedy show**

10 Run with the cool crowd on **East 6th Street**

11 See why Austin is the **"Live Music Capital of the World"**

12 Sip a **craft brew**

19 Kick back at a **drive-in** movie

41 Paint the town red at the **oldest dancehall in Texas**

47 Drink with the devil at the **Devil's Backbone Tavern**

▲ mural by Rex Hamilton

Art & Culture

④ Celebrate Austin's **festival culture**

⑬ Dive into Latin American art at **Blanton Museum**

⑯ See cutting-edge art at Austin's East Side **galleries**

㉕ Hunt for **murals**

㉗ Immerse yourself in art at **Hopscotch**

㉚ Wear a flower crown at **Fiesta**

㉜ Shop in "Little Mexico" at San Antonio's **Historic Market Square**

㉟ Stroll through **King William Historic District**

㊱ Take in art along the **River Walk**

㊲ Walk in tranquility at the **Japanese Tea Garden**

Neighborhoods & City Streets

3 Go bar-hopping along **Rainey Street**

8 Find vintage treasures in **North Loop**

10 Run with the cool crowd on **East 6th Street**

15 Check out the ever-changing **South Congress Avenue**

33 See the best of old and new San Antonio in the **Pearl District**

35 Stroll through **King William Historic District**

36 Take in art along the **River Walk**

Family Friendly

⑲ Kick back at a **drive-in** movie

⑳ Answer the **bat** signal on Congress Avenue Bridge

㉑ See the **peacocks** at Mayfield Park

㉓ Bask in the glow of **holiday lights**

㉖ Unwrap an ice-cold *paleta*

㉙ Get spooked on a **ghost tour**

㉛ Explore underground at **Natural Bridge Caverns**

㊴ Fire an apple cannon at a **fall festival**

㊻ Step back in time at **Dinosaur Park**

㊽ Fly through the trees at **Zip Lost Pines**

Only in Austin

1 Howl at the moon in **Zilker Park**

2 Learn how to **two-step** at a hoedown

4 Celebrate Austin's **festival culture**

8 Find vintage treasures in **North Loop**

11 See why Austin is the **"Live Music Capital of the World"**

14 Eat like royalty at **food trucks**

19 Kick back at a **drive-in** movie

20 Answer the **bat** signal on Congress Avenue Bridge

24 Touch the sky at **Mount Bonnell**

25 Hunt for **murals**

Only in San Antonio

- ㉖ Unwrap an ice-cold *paleta*
- ㉘ Eat **tacos** for all three meals
- ㉚ Wear a flower crown at **Fiesta**
- ㉜ Shop in "Little Mexico" at San Antonio's **Historic Market Square**
- ㉞ Bike the **Mission Trail**
- ㊱ Take in art along the **River Walk**

1 Howl at the moon in Zilker Park

Outdoor Adventures • Get on the Water •
Family Friendly • Only in Austin • Best in Summer

Why Go: Experience a hot summer night in true Austin fashion. Watch the sun set with a picnic on Zilker Park's Great Lawn, then cannonball into Barton Springs Pool for a night swim.

Where: Zilker Park • 2100 Barton Springs Rd. • https://austinparks.org

Timing: The sun sets late in Austin during the summer so be prepared to go straight from the park to the pool, since night swimming starts at 9pm daily all summer long. Full moon swims are popular and rowdy, prompting capacity limits and admission fees. Be inside the pool gates by 8:30pm to make the headcount cut-off.

Pups zoom by but the clouds crawl at sunset in Zilker Park. The summer day just got bearable as the heat starts to wane, but there are still blanket sun bathers baking in the last of the rays. Pause from taking in the sinking sun to look behind you. Framed perfectly against the park, the Austin skyline shines in the east, as the last bit of sun turns everything golden.

It's hot and the days are long in the summer, but that's perfect. Grab a bag and stuff in a picnic blanket, swimsuit, and towel. You'll have time to make the night swim next door at Barton Springs after a sunset dinner on the Great Lawn. If you enjoy raw animal expression, plan this evening for the night of a full moon. On that night, tradition dictates that everyone at Barton Springs must howl like a wolf. The springs and the park are quintessential Austin. The howling is too.

If you don't want to pack your own dinner, head over to the food trailers across from the park and order food to attack on the lawn. At **The Picnic** (1720 Barton Springs Rd., www.thepicnicaustin.com) a handful of food trailers circle their wagons. **Coat and Thai** serves saucy Thai entrees in foil pouches with rice or noodles. Try the crab rangoons or the sweet Pad-Peanut Sauce. **Cannone Cucina Italiana** serves fresh pasta and sandwiches on focaccia bread that satiates carb-lovers. Carbonara swims in a runny, yolky yellow sauce I want to lick

 Barton Springs Pool at night

twilight at Zilker Park

sunset over Zilker Park

off the plate. **The Mighty Cone** serves crunchy battered chicken, shrimp, and avocado in a flour tortilla with coleslaw. Keep in mind there's a daily dinnertime rush, so be prepared to wait at least 15 minutes to get your food. Once your dinner is in hand, head to Zilker Park to watch the sunset.

Zilker Park's **Great Lawn** is a perfect picnic post. A flat space surrounding a big rock outcropping and lined with oak trees, the lawn has the added bonus of city skyline views that are stunning. The people watching is top notch, too. From your piece of lawn, take in the volleyball players, the yogis, and the kids biking by. Music floats past from portable speakers, and dancers deftly maneuver light-up hula hoops and flaming rope darts. Most people are doing what you're doing—hanging out on blankets to watch the sunset. A peaceful green space in the city center, Zilker sees an impromptu community gathering each evening. Keep an eye out for rogue frisbees sailing past and friendly dogs coming to sniff hello. The golden, glowing pink sunset is a bonus.

A rejuvenating night swim lies a short walk away at **Barton Springs Pool** (2131 William

▲ Barton Springs Pool

Barton Dr., 512/974-6300, https://austintexas.gov). Simply cross Barton Springs Road and head up the hill to find the entrance just south of the big lawn. Spring-fed, the three-acre pool is open for daytime swimming year-round, but from April 30 to September 30, the lifeguards leave at 8pm and the pool stays open for one last hour of frolicking under the stars. At 9pm, admission fees are waived, except for on full moon nights when fees are charged ($5 for adult residents, $9 for visitors) and capacity is limited to the first 750 people. There are changing rooms by the entrance, a diving board around the other side, and grassy lawns for bonus lounging. The deep end plunges 18 feet in some parts. Do yourself a favor and just jump in. Getting in slowly is torture, but once submerged, the 68-70 degree water feels great. Remember, this is a living spring with different types of fish darting around, a few turtles, and some sensitive and utterly adorable salamanders.

You've been licked by a dog in Zilker Park. You've been nipped by a fish at Barton Springs. You have howled at the moon with a bunch of wild animals. You're dripping and tired from swimming on a hot summer night. Congratulations, you are officially keeping Austin weird. Please pick up your trash to help keep Austin beautiful.

Connect with . . .

④ Celebrate Austin's festival culture
⑭ Eat like royalty at food trucks
⑮ Check out the ever-changing South Congress Avenue

2 Learn how to two-step at a hoedown

Nightlife • Only in Austin

Why Go: Beginner-friendly two-step lessons bring out the dancin' fool in everyone. Cut a rug to a live band and show your moves off afterwards.

Where: Broken Spoke (3201 S Lamar Blvd., Austin, 512/442-6189, www.broken-spokeaustintx.net), The White Horse (500 Comal St., Austin, 512/553-6756, www.the-whitehorseaustin.com), Sagebrush (5500 S Congress Ave., https://sagebrushtexas.com)

Timing: Two-step lessons are one hour long, beginning at 7 or 8pm, depending on the hosting bar. The days are also subject to change, so call ahead or check the bars' social media pages that week. A live country-western band usually plays immediately after each lesson; plan to stay and test out your new fancy footwork.

So, you have two left feet. That's OK. Austin bars do the Lord's work by teaching absolute beginners to scoot across the dance floor with grace. The city has deep country roots, of course,

▲ The White Horse

but every weekend brings a new city mouse who has never learned to quick-quick slow-slow, that basic two-step routine essential to shuffling around to twangy songs about love and heartbreak. Those mice can take lessons here and, with any little amount of courage, storm the dance floor in the correct position without interrupting the experts as they twirl in perfect time.

First things first: dress the part. Wear those cowboy boots you spent $300 on. Or any boot, really. Barring those, wear any close-toed shoe so your feet might survive if stepped on by a well-meaning dance partner. Throw on the denim. In Austin, blue jeans are the right outfit for anything but floating the river. Do you have a cowboy hat? Wear it if you feel confident, but it's not essential. If you must have one, choose lighter material; felt will make you sweat. You're ready!

Did I mention lessons? Sign up at an early hour to learn with other plebeians, so no one else will see you trip over your own feet. Rooted in the foxtrot, this historic dance was first

▲ enjoying live music at Broken Spoke

▲ Vanessa Vaught and Josh T. Pearson, instructors at Sagebrush

▲ Broken Spoke

called the *"valse a deux temps"* but "two-step" was ultimately catchier. You'll need a partner so bring a friend, but be prepared to switch partners throughout the lesson. You'll stand facing your partner with your left arm around their shoulder or waist (generally shoulder for ladies and waist for men) and your right arm up and out from your body. Some instructors ask you to get very close, leaning your body weight into your partner, while others let you dance with space between you. Shift your weight confidently and slide around the floor in a counterclockwise circle to the tune of Dale Watson, Carson McHone, or Mike and the Moonpies. Slow, inexperienced dancers should stick to the center of the circle. The better dancers will move faster around the perimeter. That's good etiquette, but realistically you will end up maneuvering with people of all speeds, so watch out and try not to kick anyone. Step between your partner's feet; that'll help.

Crowds include people of all ages. Once the bands start playing, spectators just milling around on the edge of the dance floor will be asked to dance. Prices for lessons usually range from free to cheap, but some venues also have cover charges, especially when live bands are playing. Be sure to check in advance.

Broken Spoke, The White Horse, and Sagebrush are three honky-tonk bars serving up dance classes. They all serve food too, so you can have dinner there before hitting the dance floor. **Broken Spoke** on South Lamar offers excellent hour-long lessons for $8 from Wednesday through Saturday starting at 8:30pm. Expect to dance pasted to your partner and to really nail the fundamentals. Open since 1964, this venue has hosted Willie Nelson and saw the rise of outlaw country and cosmic cowboy progressive country with heroes like Jerry Jeff Walker in the 1970s. It's kept its old country charm amid the high-rises springing up around it. An indoor dance floor with low ceilings is set at the back of the hall, with lots of tables for beer drinking and chicken-fried steak eating. Day one fans are a loyal clientele. A crowd of real country music lovers frequents the place, but everyone is welcome for a small cash cover.

The White Horse on the east side offers free lessons a couple times a month at 7pm, usually on a weekday. Check their website to get the latest information before you go. Crowds skew younger and see plenty of overflow from East 6th street bar-hoppers, so this isn't a typical country music dancehall. Expect a bigger beer selection and space to roam inside and on an outside patio. Bands here include local stars like Carson McHone playing excellent sets tucked into a corner in front of a red curtain. It's a great place to bring out-of-town friends.

Sagebrush on South Congress Avenue is owned by some of the folks behind The White Horse, but it's newer and bigger. For a $5 suggested donation, lessons every Wednesday at 7pm will encourage you to switch partners, but you don't absolutely have to. The top-notch instructors standout for teaching both men and women how to spin their partners, with some cool options for getting out of a "cuddle" step where you dance side-by-side. Sagebrush has high ceilings and a row of chandeliers over the dance floor inside, with a handful of pool tables and lots of seats. Their jukebox plays country-western gold, and the big backyard dirt patio has food trailers and tons of tables, making it one of my favorite hangouts. Bands range from country-western on Wednesday nights to metal to blues.

Even if you can't dance, you can walk along through a two-step. As local country musicians fire up the dance floor with ease, even your shyest friends will find themselves dancing circles around the wood floors. Check your inhibitions at the door. Mike and the Moonpies said it best: You look good in neon.

Connect with . . .
⑤ Taste Texas at addictive barbecue joints
⑩ Run with the cool crowd on East 6th Street
⑫ Sip a craft brew

Go bar-hopping along Rainey Street

Nightlife • Sip Something Strong • Neighborhoods & City Streets • Only in Austin

Why Go: The 20-something party crowd runs the show at casual, stylish patio bars in historic bungalows just south of downtown Austin, where cocktails are expertly mixed and diverse food offerings are a treat worth venturing out for all on their own.

Where: Rainey Street between River Street to the south and Driskill Street to the north

Timing: The best time to visit Rainey for a party crowd is on the weekend, but weekdays are great for casual dinner and drinks.

With dozens of unique bars all within a few minutes of each other, Rainey Street is a bar-hopper's dream. This city block of bars and restaurants was built on the bones of historic bungalows from the 1930s. Today, those little houses have been turned into polished watering holes, with more high-rises going up regularly, but it's the small reminders of the past that draw people in. It's also the ample open-air patio space at every bar, the cocktails, delicious food, live music, and food trailers sprinkled throughout. The following stops are organized by location, moving from south to north, but with everything so close together, it's easy to hop from place to place in whatever order the night takes you.

Take your pick of 54 Texas beers on tap at **Craft Pride** (61 Rainey St., 512/428-5571, https://craftprideaustin.com). Half pint pours are my favorite way to taste more than one beer on a lightweight's tolerance while listening to local bands. In the backyard patio, Austin taco purveyor **Taco Flats** (https://tacoflats.com) serve up Mexico City style tacos on house-made corn or flour tortillas. The trendy, tender birria style beef taco in a lightly fried tortilla with a side of dipping broth, or consume, is a must. As an added bonus, visit on Tuesday evenings for $1 off tacos.

A little further down the road, find the glowing, hot pink mini food truck, **Little Lucy's** (424/235-8297, https://littlelucys.com). Hot, fresh mini donuts rolled in flavored sugars like

1: Craft Pride's back patio **2:** beer on tap at Craft Pride **3:** Little Lucy's **4:** Bungalow

pumpkin spice, horchata, and butterscotch and bourbon are a magnet for the bar crowd looking for scrumptious calories.

Step into **Lucille** (77 Rainey St., 512/322-9270, http://lucilleaustin.com/index.html) for the dark booths and sheer red curtains inside. Booth space is scant, so you'll likely stand inside, but romantic vibes drip from the flower draped chandeliers. Dark wood floors and enchanting booths aside, the music is loud and funky, and I almost always end up on the back patio anyway. Try a wasabi Bloody Mary for a punchy pick-me-up.

A couple steps north, the best sausages in Austin are served at **Banger's Sausage House & Beer Garden** (79, 81, & 81 ½ Rainey Street, 512/386-1656, www.bangersaustin. com). Their sausages are hand cut, hand seasoned, hand ground, hand linked, and sometimes hand smoked. Plus, they have veggie options like their Vegetarian B.L.T. with sun-dried tomato sausage stuffed with cheese curds. Try their gravy-drenched poutine with a brat or currywurst and eat at the long family-style tables in the back. More than 60 beers are on tap, too.

Cross over to the west side of the street and you'll find that a handful of food trucks have circled their wagons. Trailers sometimes change, but keep an eye out for **Burro Cheese Kitchen** (80 Rainey St., 512/565-1963, www.burrocheesekitchen.com) selling gourmet grilled cheeses, like Gouda and Provolone on sourdough with swipes of balsamic apricot fig sauce. **Four Brother Venezuelan Kitchen** (80 Rainey St., 512/554-5650, www.fourbrothersatx. com) slings *apreas,* little corn pockets of succulent meat fillings, and empanadas, similar but wrapped in bread.

At **Icenhauer's** (83 Rainey St., 512/473-0005, www.icenhauers.com), live music is a staple. The 10-piece soul band The Nightowls plays every Sunday, and DJ EYE Q often rocks the patio with an African and Caribbean mix she calls "Island Soul." Try "The Kelsey," a mint infused vodka cocktail with peach puree. Next door, **Idle Hands** (85 Rainey St., www.idle-handsaustin.com) hosts live singer-songwriters daily, and their own great food menu offers Cuban sandwiches, plantain chips, and chorizo-infused burgers. Try one of their Cuban draft cocktails, like the rum, banana, amaro, and bitters combo called "There's Always Money." For a casual drink without a big crowd, duck into the corner space called **Little Brother** (89 Rainey St., www.littlebrotherbar.com) and order a "boilermaker" (a beer and shot combo).

My favorite bar is the **Drafting Room** (88 ½ Rainey St., 512/626-8411), a long, gravel-covered space lined with bamboo with a few chairs and prosecco on tap. Local techno crews are known to have monthly sets in the space, but check the schedule ahead of time. Down the sidewalk, **Container Bar** (90 Rainey St., 512/320-0820, https://dunlapatx.com/container-bar) is a maze constructed out of recycled shipping containers. With live music every weekend and tasty cocktails, it's a hotspot with lines down the block second only to the lines at **Bungalow** (92 Rainey St., 512/363-5475, www.bungalowaustin.com). A huge covered back porch and DJs frequently playing rap and electronic music draw people in at Bungalow. The "I hate you so much" mural lives here, the cheeky antithesis to the iconic "I love you so much" mural. **The Alibi** (96 Rainey St., https://alibiaustin.com), a casual sports bar, features Detroit-style Sicilian pizza from Via 313 Pizza. Order the Cadillac to taste apricot preserves layered with prosciutto and drizzled in a balsamic glaze.

Make a point to stroll through this area to enjoy this bit of history before it's gone forever. **Lustre Pearl** (94 Rainey St., 512/469-0400, https://dunlapatx.com/lustre-pearl-rainey) has plans to bring back it's small mezcal room, Bar Illegal, as a basement bar. Should it be up and running by the time you're there, and you're lured in by the custom cocktails made to your tastes by the skilled bartenders, remember that there was once a small house where there is now a large, two-story enterprise and think about how quickly things change.

Connect with . . .

2 Learn how to two-step at a hoedown

10 Run with the cool crowd on East 6th Street

11 See why Austin is the "Live Music Capital of the World"

14 Eat like royalty at food trucks

25 Hunt for murals

4 Celebrate Austin's festival culture

Only in Austin • Art & Culture

Why Go: ACL and SXSW music festivals are iconic, but the local festival scene runs deeper than you might imagine. You'll find there are a lot of ways to experience live music, literature, dancing, food, and quirky Austin-only holidays.

Where: Festivals take place throughout the city. For an overview of upcoming events, check www.austintexas.org or www.austinchronicle.com.

Timing: Austin festivals happen year-round. Some are single day events while others stretch across multiple weekends. Buy tickets and arrange lodging, if necessary, well in advance, especially for big events like ACL and SXSW.

Festivals are a big deal in Austin, and the city's calendar is packed full of them. For decades, Austinites have nurtured these events, celebrating the city's fun-loving atmosphere, overflowing talent, and joyful weirdness. Music festivals are numerous but far from the only game in town. Whether you're looking for new bands, poets, or ways of celebrating art, Austin has a festival for you.

Take the behemoth **Austin City Limits Music Festival** (ACL; www.aclfestival.com). From a 42,000-person weekend festival in 2002, the musical event of the season now draws upwards of 450,000 people to a three-day party now held twice, on two consecutive weekends each October in Zilker Park. The whole kit and caboodle started as a way to showcase bands that played on the Austin City Limits television series, a showcase of country, rock, folk, and Americana. That was then. Today's packed lineups include rap stars, Latinx musicians, pop music, and electronic bands.

Another toast of the town, **South by Southwest** (SXSW; www.sxsw.com) kicked off in 1987, founded by local alternative newspaper The Austin Chronicle and Austinites like Nick Barbaro and Louis Black. The full week of music events downtown every March is a whirlwind of nearly 2,000 acts spanning all genres, and that's only the tip of the iceberg. There are separate "tracks" and tickets are available for film, comedy, and gaming portions, with speakers and

▲ revelers at Carnaval Brasiliero

▲ Kite Festival

▲ Austin City Limits Music Festival

conferences held downtown. The music portion launched the careers of musicians like John Mayer and pushed The White Stripes forward into fame, but the week is a boon even for people who can't afford a wristband to see the big-name headliners. Every manner of events, paid or free, sanctioned or renegade, pop up throughout the city that week.

Carnaval Brasiliero (http://sambaparty.com) is a one-day dance party just before Lent. It has become a late February bacchanal for samba lovers. Attendees come dressed as if it were Brazil in February (where temperatures reach the high 80's). Wild costumes are encouraged; the bigger the headdress the better, and sequins are de rigueur. The party was started by Brazilian students at the University of Texas in 1975, and has been bouncing around different venues each year, growing with visiting samba dancers from Rio de Janeiro, vocalists from Brazil, and lots of cocktails. The party is for those 21 and up, with plenty of Brazilian caipirinhas on the menu.

The family-friendly **Kite Festival** (www.abckitefest.org) has filled the sky over Zilker Park with colorful and creative kites since 1929. Bat kites, butterfly kites, rainbow kites, box

▲ Texas Book Festival

kites, dragon kites—they're all here. The free event is held on the first Sunday in March, and the weather can be tricky, sometimes cancelling the fun. Then there are the years that see the party press on despite the rain. It's a chance to meet the community when your kites inevitably get tangled. Kite making booths are open until 4pm for those who arrive without one.

Eeyore's Birthday Party (https://eeyores.org) is a daylong party in Pease Park on the last Saturday in April each year. An all-ages, hippie-weirdo spectacular from 11am to dusk, this festival is pure drum-circle costume vibe. University of Texas students started the tradition in 1963 and named it after Winnie-the-Pooh's Eeyore, who would get sad if he thought his friends forgot his birthday. The large, spontaneous drum circles soundtrack the groovy, sun-kissed, sometimes topless Austinites dancing in hats, beads, wigs, masks, and glitter. Over the years, live music has become part of the party, but the heart of the event is a few simple face-painting stations and throngs of people who bring bubbles to blow and blankets to sit on as they watch fellow Austinites hula hoop, happy just to be.

Looking for something literary? October's free **Texas Book Festival** (www.texasbookfestival.org), founded in 1995 by First Lady Laura Bush, is a two-day event featuring hundreds of authors, signings, readings, and interviews in and around the State Capitol. An evening Lit Crawl at local bars splits adult groups up to meet their favorite authors or see new ones around downtown, but events during the day are full of programs for children too. Each May, the free, daylong **O. Henry Pun-Off** (www.punoff.com) encourages the groans from an audience with two competitions, Punniest of Show and Punslingers, at the O. Henry Museum on 5th Street.

Connect with . . .

1 Howl at the moon in Zilker Park
11 See why Austin is the "Live Music Capital of the World"

Taste Texas at addictive barbecue joints

Taste of Texas • Only in Austin

Why Go: With over 100 years of practice in rendering tough brisket into a tender, show-stopping meal, Austin has the best of Central Texas barbecue.

Where: Citywide

Timing: For the best barbecue experience, grab a few beers and enjoy a long lunch with friends and family. Be forewarned, you might need a nap afterwards.

Welcome to Central Texas barbecue. Around here, beef is king. Big sheets of butcher paper are piled high with juicy, tender brisket. Pungent white onions, salty green pickles, spicy jalapeños,

and white bread are de rigueur. Smoked with wood, not grilled with coal, this unpretentious barbecue is enhanced with simple salt and pepper rubs instead of painted with sauce. In Austin, barbecue is revered as some of the very best of the region's cuisine.

German and Czech immigrants in Central Texas began smoking unsold meat cuts in their meat markets in the 1850s, when beef was the most plentiful and cheap protein in the state. A tough cut of meat from the chest of a cow, brisket was usually left over after the choicer cuts were ordered. The price was right, and smoked meat became the star of Central Texas barbecue for traveling cotton-pickers, cowboys, ranch

▲ nachos and brisket at Valentina's Tex Mex BBQ

hands, and roughnecks. Black and Latino cotton-pickers meanwhile started a trend of eating off butcher paper, adding other staples from meat-market shelves to their plate, creating an enduring pairing of barbecue with raw onions and pickles.

Inside Austin city limits, **la Barbecue** (2401 E Cesar Chavez St., Austin, 512/605-9696, www.labarbecue.com), which opened in 2011, is my favorite. While founder LeAnn Mueller might be the daughter of Texas' well-loved Mueller Barbecue, she and her wife, Ali Clem, run their own show here. They slow cook their brisket for 14 to 16 hours, allowing the fat to liquify

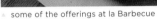
some of the offerings at la Barbecue

Valentina's Tex Mex BBQ

LeRoy & Lewis

rather than crisp up, transforming a tough muscle into a moist cut of beef (the ultimate badge of barbecue know-how). The salt balance is perfect, and the sides are spicy. The beef at la is also grass fed, hormone free, and locally sourced. Chipotle coleslaw, spicy pickles, and chipotle sausage bite back, and house-made kimchi shines beside pickled red onions. Order out of the Quickie Pickie and grab a beer while you wait, and then sit inside or take your food to go.

Franklin Barbecue (900 E 11th St., Austin, 512/653-1187, https://franklinbbq.com), home to James Beard Award winner Aaron Franklin, famously draws lines around the building and down the block. Since 2009, Texans have happily queued for Franklin's "till-we-sell-out" style operation (usually around 2 or 3 pm), drinking from six-packs chilling in a cooler at their feet while they wait. Franklin also claims antibiotic-free beef, which is said to do things in a smoker that conventional brisket couldn't dream about. Brisket is served fanned like a deck of cards to show off the beautiful brine and moist pink meat. Grab a bourbon banana pie for dessert. There are few crowded tables inside and on the patio, but the experienced take their food to go. If you're really wowed, check out Franklin's pitmaster Master Class or best-selling books. Aaron Franklin has also won *Texas Monthly's* Best Barbecue Joint in Texas award, as well as Bon Appetit's Best Barbecue Joint in America.

True to the great food truck culture in Austin, there are more than a couple of excellent barbecue trailers to choose from as well. On Sundays, **Kerlin BBQ** (2207 E Cesar Chavez St., Austin, 512/412-5588, www.kerlinbbq.com) in East Austin serves amazing kolaches, a puffy dough pastry filled with brisket and cheddar you'll want to try with a side of pinto beans.

Valentina's Tex Mex BBQ (11500 Manchaca Rd., Austin, 512/221-4248, www.valentinastexmexbbq.com), founded in 2013, embraces barbecue and Tejano cooking from the heart. Founder and pitmaster Miguel Vidal is a San Antonio local and proud Mexican-American with a lifetime of food service experience from a family of restauranteurs. Breakfast tacos like the Real Deal Holyfield are a must-try, which adds brisket to a traditional Tex-Mex breakfast of eggs, beans, bacon, and salsa all into a homemade flour tortilla. Berkshire pork mesquite-smoked carnitas tacos with caramelized onions, cilantro, lime, and habanero salsa on the side are definitely comfort food.

Relative newcomers **LeRoy & Lewis** (121 Pickle Rd., Austin, 512/945-9882, https://leroy-andlewisbbq.com) opened in 2017 and serve from a trailer at Cosmic Coffee off of South Con-

Celebrate

Every November, the ***Texas Monthly* BBQ Festival** (www.texasmonthly.com) features the best smoked meats in the Lone Star State. Ticket-holders sample as much BBQ as they want from pitmasters on the *Texas Monthly* Top 50 BBQ Joints in Texas list. From the front steps of the Long Center for the Performing Arts overlooking Auditorium Shores, enjoy succulent brisket, ribs, sausage and more, plus live music from Western swing and Gulf Coast soul bands.

gress Avenue in Austin. LeRoy & Lewis leans into south Texas barbecue territory by offering flavorful, hearty *barbacoa*. On New Year's Day, they also serve bowls of one of my favorite childhood foods, *menudo,* a traditional Mexican soup made of a cow's stomach in a red chili broth with lots of hominy. Sides like the healthy kale Caesar slaw and the unique (for a barbecue joint) Frito Pie are stunningly good, making this trailer an outlier among straight meat-and-potatoes barbecue joints.

Austin's barbecue is more than just a carnivore's delight. Central Texas cooks and pitmasters used cooking techniques on inexpensive cuts to create a poor man's meal now recognized as some of the best food around, transcending class lines for all occasions. Local BBQ is an essential part of tasting Texas.

Connect with . . .

2 Learn how to two-step at a hoedown
10 Run with the cool crowd on East 6th Street
12 Sip a craft brew

Save a horse, ride a bicycle

Outdoor Adventures • Hike & Bike

Why Go: There is no better way to get acquainted with Austin than cycling with a crowd of sweaty bike-lovers on streets and trails you've never been on before. Bonus: It's free!

Where: Starting points for rides change throughout the week but are usually in downtown or central Austin. Check the Social Cycling Austin Facebook page to find the next location. Rides aren't always a loop, so ask the ride leader before setting off if you need help getting back to the starting point.

Timing: You should budget three to five hours for a ride, but it can be shorter if you are comfortable breaking off from the group. Weekend rides include stops for food and drinks and can take the better part of a day.

Social Cycling Austin events, held at least three times a week, feel like a parade. Don't worry: You won't need to buy skin-tight, moisture-wicking spandex shorts and a zippered jersey for this bike ride. You'll fit in better with muddy sneakers and jorts. It's casual, usually kind of sweaty, and an incomparable way to experience the city. You'll join a tight-knit community of riders who follow routes winding along city streets and unpaved trails on bikes tricked out with flashing lights. You could wind up flying through the trees on a dirt path on your way to have some beers or Topo Chicos in a park, or jumping into a spring-fed pool.

Fellow riders range in age and abilities from novice to expert, representing a wide cross-section of the Austin population. There's plenty of time to hang out and get to know the other cyclists, and everyone is welcoming and supportive. On one of my first visits, I rode with the group on a fancy borrowed bike and was struggling to keep up on a beautiful, paved trail when a sweet woman gracefully sailed past me and said, encouragingly, "You'll get the hang of it once you learn how to use your gears."

Social Cycling Austin hosts several weekly themed rides. You can't miss the large glow-in-the-dark crowd that gathers for the **Thursday Night Social Ride** at Festival Beach on Lady Bird Lake at 7:30pm. The **Saturday Morning Caffeine Cruise** usually starts some-

▲ riding into Austin

▲ night ride on the Hike-and-Bike Trail

▲ bike riders gathering for an evening ride

cycling near the Capitol building

where you can order coffee and breakfast, like the Tamale House, before heading somewhere cool: a local art collective, a farmers market, or a fun Austin landmark. The **Yoga Ride** meets on Tuesday evenings and includes an outdoor yoga class led by a local teacher. On hot summer days, it ends with a dip in Barton Springs to cool off. The **Bikin' Betties** ride is a beginner-friendly, ladies-only ride on Monday nights. The **Full Moon Ride** goes out around midnight once a month.

Most of the rides take about three to five hours, including stops to grab a drink and hang out. You can always cut out early if you know where you are, but if you don't, you'll never be left behind. Ride leaders do a great job pacing the ride for all levels and keeping experienced people in front of and behind the group. A local photographer often snaps photos while he leads the ride. You'll learn how to safely signal for cars and eventually feel pretty cool yelling "Car back!" to warn everyone to ride away from the car lanes.

"BYOB" here means Bring Your Own Bike (though don't forget to bring water, too!). But it's okay if you don't know the difference between a gear bike and a fixie. As long as you can ride it, you'll be fine. In the market for a bike? At Austin's **Yellow Bike Project** (1216 Webberville Rd., 512/524-5299, https://austinyellowbike.org), you can work in their shop to eventually earn one for free, or you can rent a bike at **Trek Bicycle** (517 S Lamar Blvd., 512/477-3472, www.trekbikes.com). If you are an aficionado, you'll find your kind here, too.

In terms of flair, more is more at Social Cycling Austin events. Bike lights are key for safety, but local bikers have turned them into an art form. Bike frames are wrapped with flashy LEDs in gorgeous shades of blue and pink. Even fur-babies along for the ride have lights on their carriers. Be sure to look up and say hi to Blake. He's the one on the really, really tall bike. He does fall down at times, and he's got the dental bills to prove it.

Connect with . . .

1 Howl at the moon in Zilker Park
5 Taste Texas at addictive barbecue joints
12 Sip a craft brew

Laugh your heart out at a comedy show

Nightlife • Art & Culture • Only in Austin

Why Go: The local comedy scene is an objectively fantastic, highly dedicated, hilarious group of moonlighters, seasoned professionals, and smart college kids. Comedians are honing their craft nearly every night of the week in local cafés, breweries, and comedy clubs across Austin.

Where: Look up your favorite coffee shop or brewery—chances are they have a free comedy night. For established comedy houses with a cover (usually), try the beloved Cap City Comedy Club, The Creek and the Cave, or Fallout Theater.

Timing: Throughout the city, comedy shows range from a hard one-hour cutoff to several hours for local showcases. Some large clubs serve dinner and drinks, and a lot of breweries and cafés do too, so get there with enough time to order before the show starts. Wednesday night is especially popular for free showcases, often featuring the headliners who will play a ticketed room on Friday or Saturday.

Years ago, I found a free Saturday night comedy showcase called **Sure Thing** in the back of the Austin Java on South Lamar. Chairs packed a room with two glowing arrows suspended above and pointed at a mic on a small stage. The dimmed room filled to standing-room only for a rotating lineup of five or more comics doing their best set or trying out new material every week. The crowd roared, whimpered, giggled, and howled. I went to Sure Thing religiously with my boyfriend. After we broke up, I went alone. I took my rebound dates. I took friends who visited from out of town. Mixed bag that it was, every night was worth it. Eventually, I noticed that other venues had comedy nights, too.

The caliber of Austin comedy is high all year round. A diverse group of local comics—men, women, non-binary, straight, gay, young, and old—get out there and do the work to try out new jokes, bomb, tweak them, and try again. To orient you, a few great Austin talents include, just off the top of my head: Andrew Dismukes, a baby-faced student from the University of Texas who became a featured cast member on *Saturday Night Live;* Martha Kelly, who co-starred with Zach Galifianakis and Louie Anderson on FX's *Baskets;* Maggie Maye, who was on Conan;

Sure Thing hosts Brendan K. O'Grady and Duncan Carson

Vanessa Gonzalez at The Creek and the Cave ATX

Angelina Martin and Carlton Wilcoxson hosting Buzzkill at the Buzz Mill

▲ Fallout Theater

Daniel Rugg Webb, who has toured with Margaret Cho; and Chris Tellez and Chris Cubas, who appeared on Comedy Central.

While the comedy scene is ever changing, the options are endless. Nowadays Sure Thing runs weekly at the **Fallout Theater** (616 Lavaca St., 616/676-7209, https://falloutcomedy. com). Open-mics at the **Spider House Ballroom** (2906 Fruth St., 737/990-9562, https:// spiderhouseatx.com) see dozens of comics show up to put their names on a list and wait for a slot. Buzzkill at the **Buzz Mill** (1505 Town Creek Dr., 512/547-9909, www.buzzmillcoffee. com), a lumberjack-themed bar, is no less packed, with hushed shushing of the regular bar crowd talking near the covered stage area. Musical sketch comedy and vaudeville at **Esther's Follies** (525 E 6th St., 512/320-0198, www.esthersfollies.com) is a weekly political riot of modern-day vaudeville and a great night out. At **Cap City Comedy Club** (11506 Century Oaks Terrace, Austin, www.capcitycomedy.com) look for national headliners and the Funniest Person in Austin contest. Pro-tip: qualifying rounds are absolutely worth attending. You will spit

Celebrate

The **Moontower Comedy Festival** highlights the best of the best and is one of the shining jewels in the city's festival crown. Spilling across two or three weekends in September, the festival events take place in theatres throughout the city. It curates a diverse lineup, with past headliners including Hannibal Buress, Margaret Cho, Amy Schumer, Maya Rudolph, Leslie Jones, Tiffany Haddish, Hasan Minhaj, and Bill Burr. Check the website (https://www.austintheatre.org/moontower-comedy) for exact times and details.

your drink out with laughter. **The Creek and the Cave** (611 E 7th St., Austin, 737/222-0852, www.creekandcave.com) is a local outpost of a New York comedy favorite.

A lot of the work in Austin's buzzing comedy scene is done for free or cheap, simply because the locals want to share their work. After a comedy show, one great way to support a comedian is by following them on social media. This helps raise their profile. And as always, don't forget to tip your bartender.

Connect with . . .

12 Sip a craft brew
14 Eat like royalty at food trucks

Find vintage treasures in North Loop

Neighborhoods & City Streets • Shopping • Only in Austin

Why Go: Pearl snaps, polka dots, and patio tables from your cool grandma's collection are among the funky finds vintage shops offer in this stylish older Austin neighborhood.

Where: Along North Loop Boulevard, between Chesterfield Avenue and Avenue F

Timing: Shops typically open at 11am or noon and close between 5pm to 8pm. Some places close one or two days a week, so check ahead if your heart is set on a certain store. Otherwise troop out earlier on any day to pick through vintage treasures at your leisure.

We like vintage in Austin because we know it's eco-friendly with maximum flair. Worldwide vintage crawlers know the prices here are *très* reasonable, and locals flock to the cool second-hand shops in droves. Safari through the flora and fauna on prints of yesteryear for a guaranteed fresh find. Don't forget your reusable shopping bag when you visit this cluster of cool in North Loop.

▲ Blue Velvet

Austin's North Loop is a hip, neon-loving but relaxed district. Shops are mostly local, homegrown affairs covered with murals and funky artwork and offering style by the pound. Parking lots for this area are small and sometimes tight, but the residential streets are easy to station on if you need more room. Keep your eyes open as you find your way to this gem of a neighborhood. Austin's little treasures reveal themselves in unexpected places.

Blue Velvet (217 W North Loop Blvd., 512/452-2583, www.bluevelvetaustin.com) has been a part of the Austin community for over twenty years and is the go-to for funky, stand-out vintage frocks and frills. Dresses are helpfully organized by decade, with tailored 50s dresses near quilted 60s and floral 80s styles. Find vintage purses and one-piece swimwear alongside modern splashes like gummy bear earrings. Next door, get hip to the beat of the far-out scene

Breakaway Records

Forbidden Fruit

Room Service Vintage

at **Breakaway Records** (211 W North Loop Blvd., 512/538-0174, http://breakawayrecord-shop.com). Music here includes affordable used vinyl LP's and 45's from 1920s to today along with vintage turntables and accessories. The records here are categorized with conventional labels as well as being sorted into "Guilty Pleasures," "Rainy Day Music," "Date Night," and "Gift Ideas."

Keep an eye out as you head east on North Loop Boulevard to get to the rest of the shops. I passed a cute, crocheted snail bombed onto a chain link fence on a recent trip. Pick up some college-town intellectual simulation at a volunteer-run anarchist bookstore focused on economic and social justice, **Monkeywrench Books** (110 North Loop Blvd. E, 512/766-6925, www.monkeywrenchbooks.org). It also serves as a community hub, hosting film screenings and reading groups. Browse the shelves, drop off supplies to be distributed to houseless populations, or volunteer to work in the bookstore if you'd like to learn more.

▲ Big Bertha's
Paradise Vintage

For friskier individuals looking to cast aside the stigma and shame that goes with learning about sexuality, **Forbidden Fruit** (108 North Loop Blvd. E, 512/453-8090, https://forbiddenfruit.com) is the place to be. Over 40 years ago, this North Loop mainstay was originally established as a gag gift shop. Today, the women-owned shop offers monthly fun, funny, and informative lecture-based sex exploration workshops, as well as a modern inventory of all the newest toys. The shop has a wide-open feel with items displayed on racks mounted to soft-pink painted walls, a hat stand piled with feather boas, and friendly helpful employees.

For more conventional shopping, find **Big Bertha's Paradise Vintage** (112 North Loop Blvd. E, 512/444-5908) next door to Forbidden Fruit. Dripping in glam, this shop specializes in special-occasion vintage in a small room packed with fancy garments and prestige labels. Louis, Gucci, Fendi, Prada—the gang's all here.

Across the street, **Ermine Vintage** (106 North Loop Blvd E, 512/419-9440) and **Room Service Vintage** (117 North Loop Blvd E, 512/451-1057, https://roomservicevintage.com) have more diverse moods of vintage, from cozy to costume. Ermine Vintage does us all the favor of organizing clothing by modern day size, and not label size, so no more wondering if a 1970s Large sweater would look good on your toy poodle. Room Service is a small maze of furniture, knick-knacks, and boots. An anchor on the block, located in the same old pharmacy space since 1981, the shop offers every manner of funky lighting fixtures, lounge chairs, and etched metal vases.

Bloody Rose Boutique (100 North Loop Blvd. W, Ste. I, 512/222-8377, https://bloody-roseboutique.com) is a dark fashion boutique with all the black apparel you need. A long, small cavern with metal roses on the wall, Bloody Rose is not just for sleek modern goths, but for metal heads and witchy-men and women, too. My favorite find here was admittedly on the lighter side of dark: pink fuzzy Baphomet house slippers. The Lord of Darkness never looked more darling. Stock up on fishnets, chokers, lace-up pants, incense, and cute knick-knacks like salt and pepper shakers in the shape of cauldrons, and say hello to the friendly owners Nikke and Sebastian.

Connect with . . .

7 Laugh your heart out at a comedy show

14 Eat like royalty at food trucks

17 Eat your way through the best farmers market in Austin

Kayak beautiful Lady Bird Lake

Outdoor Adventures • Get on the Water

Why Go: Paddle through downtown Austin with its ever-changing skyline as your backdrop.

Where: Lady Bird Lake from Tom Miller Dam to Longhorn Dam

Timing: You'll easily spend an hour in the water, but plan for at least two in case you fall in love with floating leisurely or pulling yourself through the water. Keep an eye on the clock though since rentals bill by the half-hour. Since Texas summers are so brutal, kayak in the early morning or choose spring or fall instead. Outfitter hours vary and not all are open daily, so be sure to call ahead or check online before showing up.

On Lady Bird Lake, you've either got a paddle in your hand or you want one. Drive over the Lamar or Congress bridge on a sunny afternoon, any day of the week, and you'll see the water below dotted with every color of kayak, canoe, and paddleboard.

Lady Bird Lake isn't actually a lake. It's a reservoir on the Colorado River that was dammed in 1960. It was originally used as a cooling pond for a power plant, but thanks to the gusto and early advocacy of former first lady Claudia Alta "Lady Bird" Johnson and others, the scenic "lake" is the green space we see today. Previously called Town Lake, the area was renamed when Lady Bird Johnson passed away in 2007. Today, you'll hear the body of water referred to as Town Lake, Lady Bird Lake, and the Colorado River. Whatever you call it, it's a great place to get out on the water.

Since Texas summer days feel like someone left the over door open, I recommend spring and fall for kayak adventures, but if you insist on a summer adventure, go in the morning. Whenever you choose to go, be sure to bring a hat, water, sunscreen, and a credit card, as many outfitters are cashless. Sadly, swimming isn't allowed (debris from bygone days making it a little dangerous), but the water itself is safe, so capsized boaters need not worry about any a flesh-eating bacterial urban legend. Regardless, wear clothes and shoes that can get wet. Water from the paddles runs down onto your shirt and hands and all over, so think sandals, not sneak-

▲ paddling downtown

▲ Texas Rowing Center

▲ paddling west on Lady Bird Lake

ers. Nobody likes soggy socks. Austin fashion leans towards big, chunky sandals with adjustable straps. You'll see them on sunburned feet everywhere from the grocery store to a nightclub. They are a badge of honor for locals.

The best way to explore the lake is by two-person kayak, since they are the most stable. One-person kayaks are fine if you're alone, but they can wobble quite a bit, so newbies are better served by using the buddy system. The whole area from Tom Miller Dam to Longhorn Dam outlaws motorized boats, so paddling recreationists have the run of the place. Gauge your own comfort and proceed accordingly. Should you paddle east of Interstate-35, you'll notice a small land mass in the center of the water. This is Starnes Island, or Snake Island, a submerged hill that kayakers sometimes pull up onto for a break. I've never docked, but friends have brought back reports that yes, there are actual snakes nearby.

There are four main kayak outfitters nestled along the shores of the lake: **Rowing Dock** (2418 Stratford Dr., 512/459-0999, www.rowingdock.com), **Texas Rowing Center** (1541 W Cesar Chavez St., 512/467-7799, www.texasrowingcenter.com), **Austin Rowing**

▲ kayaking on Lady Bird Lake

Club (74 Trinity St., 512/472-0726, https://austinrowing.org), and **Live Love Paddle** (1610 E Riverside Dr., 512/804-2122, www.livelovepaddle.com). Most require at least one photo ID per watercraft and rent on a first-come-first-served basis, so you don't need an advance reservation. Children are welcome as well but might be asked to wear a lifejacket. Rates for a single kayak are $15 for the first hour at each dock. Double kayaks will run $20 for the first hour, and the charge goes up by the quarter hour or half hour depending on where you rent. Lifejackets are included as part of the rental fee. Small dry pouches for your phone are available at most rowing docks. Otherwise, keep valuables in your trunk. A few businesses let you stash other items in cubbies on the shore, but they are not liable for anything lost.

Dogs are welcome at Lady Bird Lake and at all outfitters. Texas Rowing Center offers doggie lifejackets for no extra charge, and Rowing Dock offers a free second hour to kayakers with pets on Tuesdays for "Yappy Hour." You'll need to provide your own canine flotation device to bring your dog at Live Love Paddle.

On the water, learning to paddle is easier than you think, and there are five miles of water to travel if you've got the stamina. Take breaks to float around and take in the scenery. Those cottonwoods, pink redbuds, and cypress trees were planted for everyone to enjoy.

Connect with . . .
- **5** Taste Texas at addictive barbecue joints
- **12** Sip a craft brew
- **20** Answer the bat signal on Congress Avenue Bridge

10 Run with the cool crowd on East 6th Street

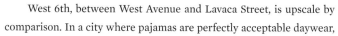

Neighborhoods & City Streets • Nightlife

Why Go: Enjoy a relaxed but vibrant nightlife with great food and small patios.

Where: 6th Street east of IH-35

Timing: Plan an evening out sipping cocktails and grabbing dinner. To shop, check store hours before you head out. While you can go out any night of the week, East 6th Street really comes to life on Friday and Saturday evenings.

Austin's 6th Street is a nightlife hub with three personalities. Each segment of this street gets the benefit of a vibrant live music scene and exceptional local food, with outdoor patios in abundance, but East 6th is my favorite stretch.

▲ Liberty Bar

With all due respect, Dirty 6th, which runs between Congress Avenue on the west and IH-35 on the east, is the rowdiest, youngest part of the street, with college-aged crowds packed like cows at a cattle drive. Bars share walls with one another, cramming the blocks with drink specials and loud music. Streets are blocked off with barricades on the weekends and mounted police officers keep an eye on the revelers.

West 6th, between West Avenue and Lavaca Street, is upscale by comparison. In a city where pajamas are perfectly acceptable daywear, this crowd is dressed to the nines. Bars are packed in less tightly, with more restaurants taking up real estate and no swarms of bar-hoppers forcing car lanes to shut down.

East 6th runs east of IH-35 to Pedernales Street and is the hip sibling of the bunch. It's a balance of casual epicurean tastes, upscale cocktails, and unkempt pool tables. Come when you're hungry, because this stretch offers as much to eat as drink.

If you need a pick-me-up coffee, start at **Cuvée Coffee Bar** (2000 E 6th St., 512/368-5636, https://cuveecoffee.com). One block east is the small contemporary art gallery **Link & Pin** (2235 E 6th St., Ste. 102, 512/900-8952, https://linkpinart.com), with rotating artists' works

RealMusic RealFashion

Hotel Vegas

Grackle

on display. For more art, continue east and check out the **murals** on 6th and Pedernales Streets. Pink and black geometric stencil work from Mexican artist Ulys Gold is a local piece by an artist with work in Marfa, Houston, and all across Austin. Cross Pedernales Street and stop in at **BLK Vinyl** (2505 E 6th St., 512/220-6536, https://blkvinylatx.com), a second-hand record shop specializing in 60s and 70s pop, rock, jazz, and R&B. Austin artist Matthew Winters painted the hypnotic black and white mural of a cat scratching a record out front.

From here, head back west a couple blocks and duck into **Whisler's** (1816 E 6th St., 512/480-0781, https://whislersatx.com) for a cocktail in their upstairs old-fashioned Oaxacan mezcal bar. For pizza, you must try **Via 313 Pizza** (1802 E 6th St., 512/580-0999, www.via313. com) and its Detroit-style masterpieces. Or head to **Lefty's** (1813 E 6th St., 737/242-7550, www. leftysbrickbar.com), a new outdoor bar with a Cajun food and lots of patio table seating. Check out the **murals** of Cesar Chavez and old Mexican gunslingers and musicians in ghostly white and turquoise by prolific Austin artist Federico Archuleta. For blow-your-mind fried chicken sandwiches, try **Spicy Boys** (https://spicyboysonline.square.site) food truck in the patio lot at **Zilker Brewing Co.** (1701 E 6th St., 512/712-5590, https://zilkerbeer.com). They also have fried tempeh burgers, papaya salads, and roti with curry.

Head across the street to shop for funky day-party or glammed-up nighttime threads at **RealMusic RealFashion** (1630 East 6th St., Ste. 104, 210/414-3450, https://realmusicreal-fashion.com), a small boutique opened by local dance music promoter power couple Kelly Gray and Andrew Parsons. Nearby, **The Liberty** (1618 E 6th St., 512/514-0502, https://theliber-tyaustin.com) and **Grackle** (1700 E 6th St., 512/520-8148) are great hole-in-the-wall bars that are worth a visit despite being dwarfed by the newer expensive buildings that crept in around them.

If you're looking for an upscale cocktail and nosh, make your way five blocks west, passing condos and cute cafés, to check out the beautifully wrought interior and patio at **Ah Sing Den** (1100 E 6th St., 512/220-0218, https://ahsingden.com). A good bet any night, it's the place to see and be seen on Thursday nights, when the city's best house and techno DJs spin records from the beautiful courtyard garden. Don't feel too bad if on the way there you're lured into the patio at **Ramen Tatsu-Ya** (1600 E 6th St., 512/893-5561, https://ramen-tatsuya.com), a favorite for Japanese soul food like rich, slurpable noodles and sake cocktails. For dessert, head to the

Celebrate

Originally named Pecan Street, 6th Street hosts the free **Pecan Street Festival** (https://pecanstreetfestival.org/) twice a year, on the first weekend in May and the last weekend in September. It's the largest arts and crafts market in Texas and has been a great reason to enjoy a turkey leg or daytime drink since 2006. Live music from dozens of local Austin bands plays across three stages and petting zoos keep kids entertained. Find the festival between Brazos Street and IH-35.

Gelateria Gemelli (1009 E 6th St., 512/535-2170, www.gelateriagemelli.com) for gelato and cocktails.

For those who don't want to stop the party, the live music at **Hotel Vegas** (1502 E 6th St., www.texashotelvegas.com) can't be beat. The venue features tons of local bands and touring acts.

More than college drinking adventures but less serious than the professional networking playgrounds you find on the other end of the road, East 6th makes for a perfect night out.

Connect with . . .

⑪ See why Austin is the "Live Music Capital of the World"
⑫ Sip a craft brew
⑭ Eat like royalty at food trucks
㉕ Hunt for murals

11 See why Austin is the "Live Music Capital of the World"

Only in Austin • Nightlife • Art & Culture

Why Go: Austin's music scene is many things—twangy, international, psychedelic, head-banging, Latin, soulful, western—and, above all, wonderfully inexhaustible.

Where: Most music venues cluster around downtown, so get to 6th Street and you can't miss. Live music abounds in bars, especially between South Congress Avenue and Comal Street. The surrounding area is part of the hot spot, with lots of concerts on Red River Street (between 6th and 11th Streets) and beyond.

Timing: Nocturnal though musicians may seem, bands often play earlier than DJs, so always check venue door times and give yourself an extra half hour to find parking and get inside the event. You can find music any day of the week, though Wednesday through Sunday is prime time. Purchase tickets in advance for bigger acts.

Lightning strikes regularly in Austin. A magnet for talent, the city's music scene has seen local musicians become stars since the '60s. And the scene still booms today, where nightly concerts and up-and-coming boutique events shine alongside world-renowned festivals.

Excellent as the music scene is, it can be overwhelming to try and find the venue that's right for you. If you don't know where to start, these three are all a good bet and range from showcasing homegrown talent to international acts. With an expansive backyard space and barbecue for sale at the bars, **Stubb's Bar-B-Q** (801 Red River St., 512/480-8341, www.stubbsaustin.com) is an unforgettable amphitheater hosting anyone from rocker Joan Jett to indie solo star Feist. The dirt space is absolutely homegrown, with a must-try Gospel Sunday brunch. **ACL Live at the Moody Theater** (310 Willie Nelson Blvd., 512/225-7999, https://acl-live.com) is a more traditional concert hall that hosts anyone from Radiohead to The Jesus Lizard, not to mention the longest running music television series, Austin City Limits. **The Continental Club** (1315 S Congress Ave., 512/441-2444, https://continentalclub.com) is a velvety red room for roots, rockabilly, country, swing, rock, and blues.

For soulful blues and jazz, venues like legendary blues club **Antone's** (305 E 5th St., 512/814-0361, https://antonesnightclub.com) offer undisputed greatness. Gary Clark Jr. even

▲ The Continental Club

▲ musicians on 6th street

▲ 6th Street during SXSW

played here early in his career. An old school marquee announces the live acts, and inside you'll find a large but intimate-feeling space with a beautiful long bar and a few tables scattered throughout. Down the street at **C-Boy's Heart & Soul** (2008 S Congress Ave., 512/215-0023, https://www.cboys.com), the Grammy-nominated soul band Black Pumas regularly pack the bar. The self-described "swankiest club on South Congress," C-Boy's has a large patio, cozy upstairs, and an iconic heart-shaped mirror over the long bar. If you're craving cool jazz in a dark cellar of a bar with dim lighting, low ceilings, and fancy cocktails, **The Elephant Room** (315 Congress Ave., 512/473-2279, https://elephantroom.com) is perfect for you...and a must-see stop for a transporting experience.

Less dedicated venues and more pop-up events, the electronic music scene is for those "in the know." Promotion companies are the most reliable way to find shows. **Exploded Drawing** (https://exploded-drawing.com) hosts monthly live electronic performances around the city. For $5 per person, the all-age shows are bathed in beautiful visual projections. **RealMusic** (www.realmusic.events) is a house, techno, and progressive DJ's daydream. Founders and power couple Kelly Gray and Andrew Parsons launched their own boutique electronic festival, Seismic, and host events nearly every weekend. Their venue, **The Concourse Project** (8509 Burleson Rd. Ste. 100), is a home for DJ events with both indoor and outdoor space.

Rock and roll will never die, and for rock music you must check out the Red River Cultural District. Stop at **Mohawk** (912 Red River St., 512/666-0877, https://mohawkaustin.com) for the coolest outdoor space in the city. An outdoor terraced space provides great views of bands like synth-trio Dallas Acid, metal band Om, and indie band Deerhunter. Take a photo by the (taxidermy) bear inside. Not downtown but worth the trip, **Emo's** (2015 E Riverside Dr., www.emosaustin.com) has morphed from a local punk freaks-and-geeks hangout to a major band touring stop. This huge box room had a small back patio for smoking and a cavernous indoor space for bands like Crosses and Chevelle.

In Live Music Capital of the World, there will always be another band that drops your jaw or changes your life just as sure as the rain falls and the lighting strikes. The well of musicians offering sounds from the soul runs deep here.

Celebrate

Live music and festivals regularly collide into a purely Austin experience. The city shines bright like a diamond when it comes time for the **Austin City Limits Music Festival** (https://www.aclfestival.com) and *The Austin Chronicle*-founded **South by Southwest** (https://www.sxsw.com), but those aren't the only highlights. **Old Settler's Music Festival** (https://www.oldsettlersmusicfest.org), now located just south of Lockhart and featuring folk, Americana, blues, and bluegrass, kicked off in 1987 as a weekend campout. Today it draws around 16,000 attendees annually. The summertime **Kerrville Folk Festival** (https://www.kerrvillefolkfestival.org), born in 1972, bills itself as the longest-running folk festival in North America. The traditionally 18-day event is a mecca for songwriters, having featured famous names like Lyle Lovett, Lucinda Williams, and Tish Hinojosa. **Austin Reggae Festival** (http://www.austinreggaefest.com) is a smokey weekend celebration on Auditorium Shores each April. November's weekend psychedelic rock and stoner-metal wizard-themed clobbering is brought to you by **Levitation Festival** (https://levitation-austin.com), currently held in venues around Austin. During summer, swarms of people descend on Zilker Park for the free **Blues on the Green** (https://www.acl-radio.com).

Connect with . . .

❸ Go bar-hopping along Rainey Street
❹ Celebrate Austin's festival culture
❼ Laugh your heart out at a comedy show

12 Sip a craft brew

Sip Something Strong • Nightlife • Only in Austin

Why Go: Over 50 breweries wait to wet your whistle in Austin. So, before you commit to another pint (or six), order a flight to help you find your new favorite brew.

Where: Citywide

Timing: Hours vary, but few breweries are open past 11pm and most close early on Sundays. Contemplative sippers should pick a weekday since weekends are busier. Check the breweries' websites to plan for events including live music, poetry readings, and other cool happenings.

Local beer fans know that Austin is home to 20 percent of Texas' craft brewers. You can visit a different taproom every weekend for a year and never repeat one. After a 20-year-long craft beer boom, the Austin beer scene has something for everyone, from imperial and hazy IPAs to creamy stouts and fruity saisons. Casual beer fans who aren't quite there yet with IPAs can easily find an approachable light ale or lager. The flight is always my first choice at a brewery, because you can choose three to five small pours of anything on tap and try that weird new sour to see how it sits with you before committing to an entire pint. Atmosphere is a big draw too, and Austin taprooms remain ever casual, often patio-rich and dog-friendly.

Let's get weird first. Twist your tastebuds at the tiny corner brewer packing a big punch with sour beers, **Blue Owl Brewing** (2400 E Cesar Chavez St. #300, 512/593-1262, https://blueowlbrewing.com). Professor Black, a sour cherry stout, is my fave, but you should try the funky Spirit Animal, a sour pale ale, too. A small taproom with a covered outdoor patio, Blue Owl is an acquired taste, but the brewers now pour the What Do You Have That's Not Sour hazy IPA and Bob's Fine Pilsner for the sour-averse.

I've been to Christian poetry readings at **Lazarus Brewing Co.** (1902 E 6th St., 512/394-7620, www.lazarusbrewing.com), and I've been there just to have beer and tacos. Lazarus is owned by a Christian pastor, which explains the poetry night, the cross logo, and the names of the beer brews like Double Predestination (a tasty double IPA), the Prodigal Pils (a refreshing

the patio at Blue Owl Brewing

beer and pie at Zilker Brewing Co. & Taproom

perfect combo of beer and tacos

the patio at Lazarus Brewing Co.

pilsner), and 40 Days and 40 Nights (the brewery's best-selling American IPA). This taproom is in the heart of the action around East 6th Street, and roll up doors let you take it all in. A room full of barrels for their special seasonal releases makes a beautiful addition.

Down the street at **Zilker Brewing Co. & Taproom** (1701 E 6th St., 512/712-5590, https://zilkerbeer.com) an old garage space is set up with tents and heat lamps in the winter, but is open to sunshine the rest of the year. Bustling no less than Lazarus despite being about half the size, Zilker offers delectable beers, like Future You, a malty temptation, and the bourbon barrel aged imperial coffee milk stout which somehow reminded me of wine. I'll admit to visiting regularly for food from the onsite Spicy Boys food trailer. Fried chicken sandwiches pair perfectly with the bready, tropical Marco IPA, but even better with the Icy Boys, a Zilker-Spicy Boys collab rice lager. Zilker joins in on the fun of hazy IPAs, serving another local collaboration beer, the delicious Foot Racer, created with Pinthouse Brewing.

Speaking of **Pinthouse Brewing** (2201 E Ben White Blvd., 512/717-0873, https://pinthousepizza.com), my favorite IPA comes from this brewpub. Reportedly named after a line

▲ a flight at Pinthouse Brewing

Celebrate

Texas Craft Brewers Festival (https://texascraftbrewersfestival.org) showcases over 75 brewers and over 200 beers each the fall. You'll pick eight beers to try for the price of admission, with the option to pony up for more refills of your four-ounce cup. Independently owned craft beer brewers from Texas are all you'll sample at this East Austin event with plenty of food vendors, DJs, and musicians.

in Wes Anderson's *The Life Aquatic*, Electric Jellyfish is an almost iridescent hazy IPA made with six different hops. A close second favorite IPA is the fantastic Training Bines. Pinthouse nails fruity, balanced IPAs, but if that's not for you, I also recommend the Mega Bloom, a sour ale with Meyer lemon, gin botanicals, hibiscus, and agave. While the Ben White location doesn't serve pizza like other Pinthouses, it has its own unique menu, ranging from pretzels and buffalo popcorn to meatball sliders and sammies. Grab a beer and a bite and enjoy the cavernous, semi open-air patio with sky-high ceilings. Better yet, go for their happy hour.

A mile and a half from Pinthouse Brewing, **Meanwhile Brewing** (3901 Promontory Point Dr., 512/308-3659, www.meanwhilebeer.com) offers tasty beers with ambiance to spare, marrying casual patios with a sleek, tiled taproom. Disco in the Panic Room and Secret Beach are Northwest and San Diego style IPAs, respectively. Their recommended pairings include ceviche and California burritos. Luckily there are food trucks on site, including Pueblo Viejo's truck which provides Tex-Mex burritos. Sprawl out in Adirondack chairs on the massive back patio and listen to live bands play funky, electronic music on a big stage.

Connect with . . .

- **7** Laugh your heart out at a comedy show
- **10** Run with the cool crowd on East 6th Street
- **11** See why Austin is the "Live Music Capital of the World"
- **14** Eat like royalty at food trucks

Art & Culture

Why Go: The largest public art collection in Central Texas is a worthwhile stop on its own. Housing the largest collection of Latin American art in the US makes a visit to Blanton essential.

Where: Blanton Museum of Art • University of Texas, 200 E Martin Luther King Jr Blvd. • 512/471-5482 • http://blantonmuseum.org

Timing: Open 10am-5pm Wednesday to Saturday and 2pm-5pm Sunday. Thursdays are free to all. Early evenings tend to be busier but it's a great way to hobnob with the local community. Reservations may be required.

Standing in the atrium of the Blanton Museum makes you feel like you're surrounded by a powerful acrylic waterfall. From a deep blue at your feet, tiles gently graduate to a foamy, faint

green high above your head. Cuban-born artist Teresita Fernández was riffing on the Blanton's architectural elements, reminiscent of the Roman Baths, and referencing Donald Judd's stacked boxes for her piece, **Stacked Waters.** The blue panels reflect light from above and darken or brighten with the movement of visitors through the space. A soothing, immersive introduction to the biggest collection of Latin American Art in the United States, Fernandez's piece bubbles like ocean water when it rushes at the shore.

▲ *Stacked Waters* by Teresita Fernández

On the second floor, Venezuelan modern artist Carlos Cruz-Diez makes you see colors that aren't actually there. Cruz-Diez's delightful, colorful body of work is represented with the 1968 piece **Physichromie No. 394,** a small arrangement of plastic strips of pink, blue, and green shades. The strips are not flat against the surface but at right angles, so that when you move around the work the colors change, reflecting but also refracting light through itself.

Not all pieces are as soothing. Some artists featured in the Latin American collection

▲ Ellsworth Kelly Chapel

▲ the Blanton Museum's modern and contemporary gallery

▲ *Stacked Waters* in the museum's atrium

highlight the cultural, economic, and political tensions of their day. In the late 1970s, conceptual work was a powerful tool in communicating ideas counter to those sanctioned by military dictatorships, where you could be killed for directly speaking out. Antonio Caro painted **"Colombia"** in a white script on a red background, just like the Coca-Cola logo, to point out the "economic and cultural colonization" of America in his country. In a dark room lit by a saintly glow, Cildo Meireles's 1987 piece ***Missão/Missões (How to Build Cathedrals)*** comments on the Jesuit's religious colonization of Brazil. Through a sheer black curtain, a wide pile of shiny copper pennies lays on the ground. A stack of communion wafers rises from the center of the pile to a canopy of femur bones lit from above. The relationship of the divine, the economic, and the bodies of the colonized is explored.

When I visited, the museum's temporary project featured mounted textiles woven by Texas-born Diedrick Brackens, a piece that explores Black and queer identity in the United States. Brackens' work embraces West African weaving traditions, creating stunning sheets of fabric that tell stories of his own life mingled with legends from Africa. His powerful piece,

Cildo Meireles, *Missão/Missões (How to Build Cathedrals)*

bitter attendance, drown jubilee, featuring two boys wading in the water with catfish is based on a Juneteenth celebration that ended with the drowning of three young Black men in America. In the piece, the men are given back to the community as catfish.

Rotating exhibits are on the first floor. An exhibit of drawings by Andy Warhol stood out to me because I had no idea he could draw. A show of classical Indian paintings I once saw was endlessly fascinating. On a recent visit, I saw sketches by old world masters, iconic images that have been copied endlessly by other artists over the years.

To stand in a rainbow, visit the **Ellsworth Kelly Chapel,** just outside the Blanton. Described as an igloo made of stucco, the chapel is laid out in a cross like a Romanesque church. Three of the arms feature colorful stained-glass installations in different formations. Something draws visitors into the light reflected by the glass inside the space, and people take turns standing in it when they visit. On the north end of the room, an 18-foot redwood totem adds another minimalistic, non-specific religious symbol further creating an inclusive and inspiring environment. Created by Ellsworth Kelly, an atheist, the chapel was envisioned as a sacred space dedicated to creativity.

Towering, white tulip-like structures will soon announce the Blanton Museum, shading the plaza. The multi-million-dollar project is set to be complete in late 2022. For now, visitors can find the entrance to the museum on Martin Luther King Jr. Boulevard and Congress Avenue, and walk around construction to visit the gift shop and café in the west building.

Connect with . . .

🔟 See cutting-edge art in Austin's East Side galleries
㉕ Hunt for murals

14 Eat like royalty at food trucks

Taste of Texas • Only in Austin

Why Go: Visit Austin's legendary food truck scene to sample endless culinary creativity and food truck brilliance as it emerges, while supporting BIPOC-owned businesses at the same time.

Where: Find food trailers and trucks all over Austin, some standing alone, and others clustered together in food truck parks like The Thicket Food Park (7800 S 1st St., http://www.thicketaustin.com), Outpost Food Park (2324 E Cesar Chavez St.), and Arbor Food Park (1108 E 12th St., www.arborfoodpark.com).

Timing: While some trucks open for breakfast, most favor a late afternoon start time and serve until they are sold out, so plan on going for dinner. Not all trucks are open daily, so be sure to check the website for hours before you venture out.

From 2010 to 2016, the salad days of food truck growth in Austin, 600 percent more trucks appeared throughout the city and trucks were known to serve better food than most restaurants.

▲ The Vegan Nom

Development has knocked some trucks out of their old spaces, and costs and regulations have gone up, but food on wheels is still stellar today. The healthy city that birthed Whole Foods serves vegan and vegetarian food you'll dream about later. Fiery Thai reimagines pre-conceived notions of what Thai food should be. New kids on the block serving Mexican street tacos sell out regularly. Austin food trucks take you around the world with flavor, proving that the food truck boom is far from over. Don't miss these exceptional meals.

The "I don't want vegan food that pretends to be meat" crowd eats their words at Austin's vegan trucks. Visit **Revolution Vegan Kitchen** (7800 S 1st St., 512/538-7318, www.revolutionvegankitchen.com) in South Austin at The Thicket Food Park. The menu offers vegan tacos made with soy and jackfruit (try the al pastor and the carnitas) and heavenly burgers like The Vaquero, a wheat protein patty stacked

▲ Dee Dee

▲ Revolution Vegan Kitchen

▲ tacos from Revolution Vegan Kitchen

with onion rings and served with seasoned curly fries. For dessert, they serve Luv Fats' dangerously good avocado-based ice cream in strawberry or chocolate-covered strawberry.

For more vegetarian options, check out **Sassy's Vegetarian Soul Food** (1403 E 7th St., 737/333-4458, https://sassys-vegetarian-soul-food.business.site). At Andrea Dawson's food truck, Chicon and Waffles are an indulgent meal made with wheat gluten, fried crispy and dipped in plain, orange, jerk, or hot lemon-pepper sauce. Balance this rich dish with a three-green medley of kale, collard, and mustard greens. On Cesar Chavez Street, Chris Rios' **The Vegan Nom** (2324 E Cesar Chavez St., 512/497-3147, www.thevegannom.com) serves tacos and burritos worth the wait. The Birdie Sanders buffalo chicken with pepper jack, onions, avocado, and cabbage would make the former presidential contender proud. Al pastor with marinated pineapple and the Planet Queso dip are simply inhalable.

Spicy flavor fiends, take note. Thai country flavors linger on your tongue at **Dee Dee** (4204 Menchaca Rd., www.deedeeatx.com), which means "Good Good," in Thai, where owner Lakana Trubiana harvests herbs directly from her own garden for the truck. Instead of curries or pad thai, Trubiana mines rustic home recipes from her home near the Thai-Lao border. Clear your sinuses with *Laab Moo,* an extremely spicy north-eastern style minced pork dish with mint, lime, and cilantro. Dee Dee is tucked in a corner behind the covered patio tables in south central Austin's neighborhood hangout, Radio Coffee and Beer. Order online ahead of time to avoid a wait.

For tacos, carnivores should not miss the hot new taco slingers, **Cuantos Tacos** (1108 E 12th St., 512/903-3918), in Arbor Food Park. Luis "Beto" Robledo serves small tacos that are big on flavor, including *suadero* (fatty, melt in your mouth beef), *longaniza* (a Spanish style sausage), and a mushroom taco that sells out quickly, to name a few. Visit their Facebook page to learn more. I braved a torrential downpour to order from Margarito Pérez's **Paprika ATX** (6519 N Lamar Blvd., 512/716-5873, https://paprikaatx.com). It was more than worth it. Try the *carnitas* (they're sous vide) and the *nopales* (cactus) with beans. The steak taco needs no accompaniment of guacamole or cheese, so try it plain. Perez's *salsa macha,* made with peanuts and skin-on garlic cloves, is out of this world.

On seafood, Austin delivers. Early-90s Cash Money Records rap blared at **Krab Kingz Seafood** (517 N Interstate Hwy 35, 512/815-1595, www.Krabkingzatx.com) on my first visit, as

I waited for a huge to-go box. The truck is an outpost of a Pflugerville sit-down Florida-style crab shop. My hefty order of crab, shrimp, corn, and potatoes was handed off with a gracious smile. Eating our feast, hands covered in buttery dipping sauce, my friends and I were convinced we needed to crack each leg with our steel water bottles, realizing belatedly that we could just break the crab legs with our hands.

And that's just the tip of the iceberg. With so many mouthwatering options to choose from, it's no wonder the food truck scene in Austin is legendary.

Connect with . . .

1 Howl at the moon in Zilker Park
3 Go bar-hopping along Rainey Street
10 Run with the cool crowd on East 6th Street
12 Sip a craft brew

15 Check out the ever-changing South Congress Avenue

Neighborhoods & City Streets • Shopping

Why Go: Stroll these two beautiful and historic Bouldin Creek neighborhood streets to sample the changing shopping scene in Austin. You'll find classic shops selling cowboy boots and candy alongside hipper places like apothecaries and up-and-coming restaurants.

Where: South of Lady Bird Lake, South 1st Street runs between Barton Springs Road to the north and Oltorf Street to the south. For South Congress Avenue, visit the heart of the area between Riverside Drive to the north and Mary Street to the south.

Timing: Shops are open from early afternoon until early evening, so plan for a weekend stroll of a few hours starting sometime around 11am to enjoy the entire experience. There's not a lot of shade on either street, so wear a hat and stay hydrated on hot summer days.

I once had a professor who asked the class to write about how much Austin has changed. That was in 2005, and today, I finally understand what he meant. The shops along South 1st Street and South Congress Avenue change often enough that if you haven't been in a while, you haven't been at all.

▲ Two Hands' patio

For something extra special, visit South Congress on the first Thursday of every month, when local merchants set up shop along the sidewalks, shops stay open until about 10pm, and restaurants will often offer drink specials.

Start on South Congress at the trendy new strip called Music Lane. Music Lane proper is the name of little street that runs behind this block to the east, but the shops are on South Congress. **Two Hands** (1011 S Congress Ave., Ste. 170, 512/215-9692, www.twohandsnyc.com) has a patio hung with pretty outdoor light fixtures and serves creative lattes. Fair warning: the beet latte is not caffeinated, but you can add a shot of espresso if you like. There are a few local shops here and quite a few larger chains, which might be what stickers refer to when they say, "Don't Dallas My Austin."

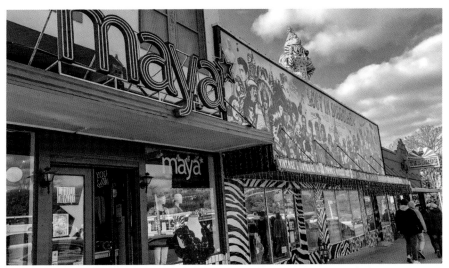

▲ Lucy in Disguise with Diamonds

▲ Art for the People

It's not unusual to see lines outside the stores. Local favorites, like **Amy's Ice Creams** (1301 S Congress Ave., 512/440-7488, https://amysicecreams.com) and **Home Slice Pizza** (1415 S Congress Ave., 512/444-7437, https://homeslicepizza.com), are definitely worth the wait.

Neighborhood Goods (1007 S Congress Ave., Ste. 120, 512/531-9050, https://neighborhoodgoods.com) is "a reimagined department store" that started in Plano, Texas. On one end of the store sits an alluring full circular bar and booths set among lush tropical plants. Further

mural by El Federico at Tesoros Trading Company

up the block, **Tecovas** (1333 S Congress Ave., Ste. 160, 512/675-4343, www.tecovas.com) sells leather cowboy boots made in Leon, Mexico. You can also grab a drink at the bar in the back.

Past Academy Drive going south, you'll come upon the older residents of South Congress. Stop into boutiques like **Risqué Nation** (2214 S 1st St., 737/209-0174, www.risquenation.com) to spend some cash on modern, edgy accessories. There are also lots of patios to choose from to stop and eat at. **Little Brother** (1512 S Congress Ave., www.littlebrotherbar.com) has a street-side window serving warm, sweet and savory kolaches in little brown paper bags. The kolaches are delicate, pillowy, and delicious.

Buy a Mexican blanket or Peruvian earrings at **Tesoros Trading Company** (1500 S Congress Ave., 512/447-7500, www.tesoros.com/homepage.html) or stop into **Big Top** (1706 S Congress Ave., 512/462-2220, www.bigtopcandyshop.com) for a candy fix. Definitely window shop at **Lucy in Disguise with Diamonds** (1506 S Congress Ave., 512/444-2002, http://lucyindisguise.com). This costume rental shop is overwhelming and tons of fun. Take a right when you get to Annie Street and walk over to South 1st.

While South 1st experiences more turnovers (shops close often and it takes a while for something new to move in), the street is still full of local personality. Some stores sit in doublewides, with a good number of old-fashioned food trailers set in little parking lots.

Charm Charm the Pug will bring you to your knees, because you have to get down there to pet her at **Art for the People** (1711 S 1st St., 512/761-4708, www.artforthepeoplegallery.com). Austin would be nothing without local artists, and you can help support over 100 of them here. Need a print of an adorably dejected robot or tea towels of cute alpacas in fringe and pom

Celebrate

A proud rainbow procession of LGBTQ+ people and allies sashay downtown every August at Austin's **Pride Parade** (https://austinpride.org). Floats with go-go dancers, queens, and cowboys stoke the celebration of love and inclusion in this all day event. The free parade usually winds from the Capitol to the Warehouse District, but check online since the route sometimes changes.

poms? Me too. AFTP is a gallery and artisan market of beautiful and affordable framed photography, prints, jewelry, ceramics and more.

If you haven't eaten yet, make a right on Annie Street and eat at **Elizabeth Street Café** (1501 S 1st St., 512/291-2881, https://elizabethstreetcafe.com), a Vietnamese and French bakery. For something vegetarian or vegan, stroll further north on South 1st to the **Conscious Cravings** (1311 S 1st St., 512/582-9182, www.consciouscravingsaustin.com) trailer. Then start making your way back south.

You'll find a few vintage shops along this street, as well as a few murals. The vintage stores are closer to the laid-back soul of Austin. Casual is the look here, and second-hand is the ethos. **Bloomers and Frocks** (1628 S 1st St., 512/582-9182, https://bloomersandfrocks.com) specializes in clothes from the 1960s and earlier. Head to the west side of Annie Street to grab a photo in front of the vibrant and highly Instagrammable mural *Greetings From Austin* by Todd Sanders and Rory Skagen. Inspired by the large letter postcards of the 40s, the mural is the essence of the area—something new, something retro, 100% Austin.

Connect with . . .

1 Howl at the moon in Zilker Park
21 See the peacocks at Mayfield Park
25 Hunt for murals

16 See cutting-edge art at Austin's East Side galleries

Art & Culture

Why Go: Community warmth runs through the local art scene. Local creators will reach out to you with open arms, flinging their home studio doors wide for your visit, plying you with beer and wine to relax and enjoy.

Where: Austin galleries are city-wide, with older established galleries on the west side and newer collectives and small galleries on the east.

Timing: Plan to spend 20 minutes at each gallery. You may need to make a free appointment by calling or going online.

Although local art blossomed with the inception of the University of Texas fine art program in the 1930s, art institutions have always been a bit smaller in Austin than in other cities. That's

▲ West Chelsea Contemporary

why intimate galleries and studios are considered the soul of art in Austin. Groups of artists clustered to exhibit together in cheap spaces come and go with rising rent prices and gentrification. The east side of Austin, an area previously considered off the beaten path for galleries, has become a hot spot. The galleries, though small, are not to be missed.

The west side, that is west of IH-35, galleries are housed in historic homes or in spaces with floor to ceiling glass wrapping the exterior. Bright, lively, and commercial, the west side of town was historically the white side of the tracks, while the east side was segregated and left trailing far behind in neighborhood investment and maintenance. Consequently, west side galleries have more established artists and fancy digs, and while some see the east side as a bit rougher around the edges, it also has a more casual, warm scene, and a colony of artist collectives.

Big Medium (512/939-6665, www.bigmedium.org), a non-profit organization that supports local artists, makes its home in East Austin at **Canopy** (916 Springdale Rd., www.canopyaustin.com), a concrete complex of studios, galleries, and offices, where it showcases

Ivester Contemporary storefront at Canopy

exhibit at Ivester Contemporary

detail of Julie Maren's installation
at Wally Workman

Passage: Variation II by artist Luke Savisky

Flight by artist
Court Lurie

contemporary work from established and emerging artists from Austin and beyond. Exhibits here are refreshingly unexpected. Steve Parker's *War Tuba Recital* was a series of fantastically assembled brass instruments you could wear. Other galleries in Canopy include other collectives, like the 20-artist group behind **ICOSA** (512/920-2062, www.icosacollective.com), which promotes "curatorial free reign," allowing artists to put on any exhibit they'd like of either their own work or work by someone they want to showcase instead. **Ivester Contemporary** (737/209-0379, http://ivestercontemporary.com) proudly showed stately portraits of Black Americans by Dave McClinton during my visit. The main space showcases contemporary work, with a "project space" in the back for more experimental pieces.

Nearby, in a 1948 Quonset hut, **Cloud Tree Studios & Gallery** (3411 E 5th St., www.cloudtreestudiosandgallery.com) is a beautiful space. The semi-circular, steel-framed structure with a big swinging porch chair out front is usually crowded with people until late at night. For one event, light artist Luke Savisky used four stacked projectors to create a strobing, dimensional but minimalistic field of hypnotic shadows on the wall for people to gaze at or play in. At another exhibit, Court Lurie, an abstract artist from Chicago, hung paintings with light colors dripping down the canvas like spills, juxtaposed with bright colors, striking shapes, and frenetic lines.

Joseph Janson's
wire work at Wally
Workman Gallery

If you want to experience the full scope of Austin's art scene, the **Wally Workman Gallery** (1202 W 6th St., 512/472-7428, www.wallyworkmangallery.com) sits in a 100-year-old-home on the west side of town. Established in 1980 and representing 53 artists from around the United States, the woman-owned gallery (Wally is a woman) mounts shows every month without fail. Incredible installations spread across two floors, like Patrick Puckett's Monsteras series featuring tropical plants surrounding confident women. And Julie Maren's raindrops imprinted in delicate patterns and acorns filled with iridescent materials cannot be done justice in photos.

Celebrate

In addition to their regular work at Canopy, Big Medium coordinates two city wide studio tours annually called the **East Austin Studio Tour** (EAST) and **West Austin Studio Tour** (WEST). EAST and WEST draw more than 50,000 attendees each year, with more than 500 artists showing off their own studios during each weekend event, one in May and the other in November. The self-guided tours are free and a great way to meet the artists that make Austin shine.

See famous street artists like KAWS, Basquiat, and Banksy, to name a few, nearby at the **West Chelsea Contemporary** (1009 W 6th St., 512/478-4440, https://wcc.art). When the former Russell Fine Art Collection opened in October 2020, they declared that the youthful city demanded an updated style, and the space now shows recognized heroes of the street art movements, reinforcing the growing importance of graffiti and creatives outside the traditional fine art sense.

Austin says hello with spectacular street art, and introduces contemporary, abstract, figurative, experimental, conceptual, and minimalist work around the city. Art-school dropouts, graduates, and self-taught creatives can show off their work here, making this smaller art scene much more than meets the eye.

Connect with . . .

25 Hunt for murals

17 Eat your way through the best farmers market in Austin

Taste of Texas

Why Go: Organic, sustainable produce is only the tip of the iceberg at this year-round farmers market where tempting hot foods and tons of little extras are gathered under a historic airport hangar.

Where: Texas Farmers Market at Mueller • 2006 Philomena St. • https://texasfarmers-market.org

Timing: Sundays, rain or shine, from 10am to 2pm, the Mueller market is open. By 1pm most vendors are packing up, so arrive earlier rather than later.

Under a big white airport hangar from 1948, the Texas Farmers Market at Mueller is like a magnet. The broad indoor space for avocado squeezers and melon sniffers bustles every Sunday morning. The produce is lush. The kale is curled. Officially, seasonal produce and supporting the local economy are why you go. However, it was the huge organic corn masa tamales from **Tamale Addiction** with bright, biting green salsa and non-traditional fillings to raise your grandmother's eyebrows (think poblano and muenster cheese or veggies and feta) that hooked me. A whole array of delicious hot foods begs you to graze. The lake, a few steps away, with a grassy hill made for picnics and a playground make for a farmers market par excellence.

a warm day at the Texas Farmers Market

I led the way through the market for my new-to-town roommate, who wore her godmother's denim overalls (no farmer relation) and carried a few canvas totes tucked neatly under her arm, ready to fill them with fruits and vegetables. But instead of heading for the carrots and cabbage, I made a beeline to the hot foods. Organic tamales were my usual go-to, but on that day we devoured **Lua Brazil's** *pão de queijo,* little spheres of warm Brazilian bread. Fresh from the oven and shiny with almost translucent spots of cheese, our three bites of tapioca-based comfort food came in regular, jalapeño, and mushroom. Hot pierogis, a type of dumpling stuffed with a combination

▲ Acorn Tea

▲ pierogis and chocolate financiers

▲ a busy market

▲ Corazon Verde Apothecary

of chicken and pork or soft potato and sauerkraut, from **Apoloni** were next. As we made our way to the other side of the market, a nice couple asked, "There's pierogis?" That couple stood in front of a booth for **Hamilton Pool Vineyards,** where we were suddenly asked to join in the wine tasting for the vineyard out in Dripping Springs. The 2019 Cabernet Sauvignon and Tempranillo were my favorites among the four wines we sampled. We could not skip dessert, so we made our way to **Luv Fats Ice Cream,** an amazingly good vegan, avocado-based desert with classic flavors like strawberry and chocolate.

Hot food (and cold ice cream) wasn't the only thing on the menu. We checked out other booths where each vendor offered samples or sniffs of their goods. Sunflower seed hummus from **Floreli** was fresh and delicious. **Corazon Verde Apothecary** offered mugwort dream salve to promote lucid dreams and astral travel according to owner Leighla Molina. Their elixirs, body oils, and teas were all made from small-batch, organic, locally sourced ingredients like reishi mushrooms and tulsi ginger. Opals and moonstones were set in sterling silver rings shaped like moons and stars at **Crystal Nova Creations.**

△ a busy market on the weekend

Sustainability is touted at this market and "producers only" means that the fruit, vegetables, meat, dairy, and other products sold at Mueller was either grown or produced with ingredients mostly from the farm you're paying. You can get everything here—your okra and your tomatoes and your multi-colored peppers and Spanish black radishes. Texas Acorn Tea is made from live oak nuts around Austin. Kombucha is a staple alongside honey wine, a sour fermented milk drink called kefir, bread, and grass-fed and pasture-raised meats and eggs. Farms from around Texas, like Johnson's Backyard and Bouldin Food Forest, stack their tables high with herbs and flowers as well as fruit and veggies.

Sitting on the grassy shore of the lake a few blocks away and eating our pierogis, my very nice new roommate forgave me for running out our time at the market with hot foods instead of shopping for produce. Content to snag a few microgreens, she wondered if we should find the juice trailer people seemed to have gotten drinks from or if we should buy fruits to make juice ourselves. We sat contentedly for a few minutes people-watching, then walked over to the adorable, 16-foot high sculpture of Nessy. Created by Dixie Friend Gray, the Loch Ness monster was mosaiced in shining green and blue handmade tiles, smiling down with glowing ocean eyes. When we looked up again, it was well after 2pm, and the market was all collapsing pop-ups and folding tables being packed away. We had missed our chance to buy any fruits. Fortunately, there's always next Sunday.

Connect with . . .

⑧ Find vintage treasures in North Loop

⑲ Kick back at a drive-in movie

18 Hike the Greenbelt

Outdoor Adventures • Hike & Bike • Get on the Water

Why Go: Feel miles from the city as you hike to a swimming hole on beautiful Barton Creek.

Where: Barton Creek Wilderness Park sprawls through southwest Austin. For information, including details about the multiple entrances, visit https://austinparks.org/barton-creek-greenbelt.

Timing: Plan two hours for a hike, with more time allowed if you plan to sit and enjoy the scenery. A creek swim is refreshing in summer, but visit early in the day before the temperature climbs to the 100s.

The Barton Creek Greenbelt has about 16 miles of trails, but I don't know anyone who wants to hike that distance when they say, "Let's go to the Greenbelt." What they mean is "Let's grab our water shoes and hike to the creek where we can drink beer, swim a little, and hang out for a few hours."

▲ a longstanding sculpture on a Greenbelt trail

The lush trails feel worlds apart from the city. The paths themselves are sometimes rocky and often narrow, and the rocks in the creeks are slippery, which explains the local sense of style. Greenbelt fashion is a pair of rubber-soled sandals with adjustable straps that create chunky sunburn patterns. During summer, hikes here are as hot as the days are long. Tote plenty of water anytime you hit the trail. You'll meet plenty of dogs, often unleashed, though usually well-behaved and on their own sniffing and scouting for adventure. Mountain bikers are trail regulars too, and it's not unusual to need to step aside so they can pass on narrow paths. Parking is free, and trailheads are often in neighborhoods.

The creeks here fill Barton Springs pool and wells throughout Texas, including the Edwards Aquifer, making Barton Creek extra sensitive and important to the entire state. Etiquette

▲ mountain biking

▲ Twin Falls

▲ views from nearby the Loop 360 trailhead

says you must never bring any glass containers to the trail, and you must always take any trash you make as you hike back out to your car.

After 15 years in Austin, I can confidently make my way to only two Greenbelt entrances without a map, but there are a lot more than that. Even if you already like visiting, chances are good that there is an access point and a watering hole that you have yet to explore.

For most of my years in the city, I hiked in using the **Loop 360 entrance** (3755-B Capital of Texas Hwy.) which is hard to miss because there are plenty of cars parked on each side of the road on most sunny days. There's a map at the trailhead to help orient you. On the trail, you're immediately rewarded with beautiful views overlooking the canyon below. The 1.5-mile trail splits off into an upper and lower portion, but they converge closer to Sculpture Falls. (Hint: It's the second big pool of water that you'll reach.) Over the years, the flowing water has smoothed the rocks and carved bathtub-like indents you can really sit in like a tub at your own natural spa. There's also a cliff nearby that people like to jump off of into the water, perfect for cooling off after a hot hike.

▲ people enjoying the water at Sculpture Falls

I've started associating my friends with different access points. Some love tackling the **Hill of Life** (1710 Camp Craft Rd.), where you have to gingerly climb a quarter mile of long white steps while trying to avoid rocks that stick into your arch and make your foot land wonky. It's another quarter mile until you get to the creek, and, if you're like me, by that time you'll be wondering if you should turn around, but you'll be too far into the hike by then. The total elevation change is about 300 feet, and hikers are often left panting. A few runners and mountain bikers will pass in their excellent cardiovascular health. The views are good, especially at sunset. At the creek where the trail levels out, a small waterfall awaits your oohs and aahs.

Other friends like to use **Gus Fruh** (2642 Barton Hills Dr.), where I was once caught along a steep rock wall in the pouring rain when trying to find a spot for a picnic. Climbers like this area, and the walls have names like New Wall and Bee Hive on the maps at the trailhead. The creek is a short 0.2-mile walk, and in the summer, it's deep enough to swim in (or sit in waist deep with a cold can and a koozie). If you're looking for more, the path connects with a mile-long trail that leads to Campbell's Hole swimming area if you take a right at your first turn in from the trailhead.

Though it's not the only Greenbelt in Austin, the Barton Creek Greenbelt is the only one with the honor of being called simply "the Greenbelt" by Austin's residents. All the trails lead to one another on this flowing ribbon through the heart of Austin, without which the city might not be the network of hikers, bikers, boulderers, trail runners and creek loafers that it is today. There's a reason Austinites are called some of the most outdoorsy people in the United States. The health of the creek is the health of the city, so keeping it clean and protected is the hard part. The trails themselves are easy, like a lazy Sunday afternoon.

Connect with . . .

🟢 Eat like royalty at food trucks

19 Kick back at a drive-in movie

Family Friendly • Nightlife • Only in Austin

Why Go: Experience a bit of nostalgia watching new indie releases and older pop culture favorites from the convenience of your car.

Where: Blue Starlite (multiple locations: 300 San Antonio St., Austin; 2015 E.M. Franklin Ave., Austin; 800 Harrell Pkwy Blvd., Round Rock; 707/374-8346, www.bluestarlitedrivein.com); Doc's Drive-In (1540 Satterwhite Rd., Buda, 512/960-4460, www.docsdriveintheatre.com)

Timing: Movies play nearly every night; go online to view showtimes and buy tickets. Budget twenty to thirty minutes over the film run time to park and grab concessions.

Drive-in movies were an American cultural moment. Consider the history. Throughout the 1950s and 1960s, thousands of screens popped up across the country. Cheap dates and gangs of friends would motor in and park under the stars. Austin's drive-in screens opened in the 1940s, just in time for the boom. After going off the map for a few decades, there was a short-lived revival in the 90s and early 2000s. Now a few Austin drive-ins are back on the radar for more than just nostalgia lovers.

Blue Starlite and Doc's Drive-In are modern drive-ins featuring throwback films, cult classics, and new releases. Lots range from mini to large depending on the location, but all offer standard concessions, like candy, cola, and popcorn. Drive-ins are a year-round experience in Austin thanks to the warm subtropical climate. Where theaters in colder cities feature in-car heaters, I was cheekily told "You can use your own in-car heater" when I asked about winter aids. Helpfully, free jump starts are offered to those in need. Tickets for movies are easy to purchase online and should be bought in advance because most theaters have limited car slots available. The sound comes in on your car FM radio, which leads to my next point.

If you ever, like me, agree to watch a horror film at a drive-in with your friends but are threatening to leave if it gets "too scary," remember: You can always turn the volume down and

decorations at the Blue Starlite

entrance at the Blue Starlite

Blue Starlite

close your eyes at the scariest parts. Although, fair warning, if you mess with the volume your friends may throw popcorn in your direction (which did not comfort me much in my case).

The **Blue Starlite** in Austin stands out because it breaks drive-in tradition. The first Austin drive-in movie theater had space for 450 cars. If that seems like a lot, the next one had space for 1000. A self-titled boutique theater, Blue Starlite's screens can only accommodate 15-25 cars, so your experience is intimate. This decade-old, homegrown enterprise started in the city and has expanded to a few different locations including ones downtown, in Mueller, and in Round Rock. The Blue Starlite resurrects films from the 1940s-1980s nightly, leaning into movies screened at real drive-ins before drive-ins first faded out. You'll see plenty of new features alongside cult classics like *Rocky Horror Picture Show, Labyrinth,* and *The Big Lebowski.* This drive-in is bring-your-own-everything, including beer and cocktails. Popcorn, sodas, and boxed candy can be ordered online with your phone.

A dusty, antique truck draped in red string lights sits between lots next to a little trailer of bathrooms at the Mueller location. Once the film starts, your car is one block in a vehicular

▲ Enjoy a movie from the comfort of your own car.

Tetris formation arranged by the attendant who waves you into your spot. This will prevent you from just driving off, but the cozy ambiance is as sweet as a box of Whoppers.

In Buda, about 25 minutes south of Austin and off a few country roads, **Doc's Drive-In** is unfussy, with a go-ahead-and-park-yourself, laid-back style. A big dirt lot in the suburbs, pickup trucks and small hatchbacks park backwards and cinephiles dangle their legs off lowered tailgates. Some families opt to watch in front of their cars in chairs with their dogs, which are allowed.

The down-to-earth ambiance belies a fancy menu, however. A vegan chicken wrap impressed a born-again vegan friend of mine, and desserts include Belgian waffles and hot brownies with Texas' Bluebell ice cream. Beer and wine are available at the on-site bar. You aren't allowed to bring your own food or drinks, but the full menu has a lot to offer.

Doc's has two big screens showing features side-by-side. They lean towards family-friendly modern movies like *Minions* and *Talladega Nights*, but 80s flicks like *The Goonies* and *The Breakfast Club* are screened as well. Scary movies are a drive-in theater classic, and you can catch titles like *The Ring*.

Drive-ins themselves are a cozy, quiet affair, but loud mouths are welcome too. Early drive-ins advertised, "The whole family is welcome, regardless of how noisy the children are." Cackle about the movie with your friends or family. No shushing is allowed, to a point. Once those windows, hatches, and tailgates swing open, all bets are off. Refunds for "the movie being too scary" are not honored. Note reader, that my friends and I survived the entire film.

Connect with . . .

🔟 Eat like royalty at food trucks

20 Answer the bat signal on Congress Avenue Bridge

Only in Austin • Family Friendly • Best in Summer

Why Go: The largest urban colony of Mexican free-tailed bats put on an awe-inspiring show at sunset, flying by the millions into the sky.

Where: Congress Avenue Bridge over Lady Bird Lake

Timing: Peak season is July to August, but you can see the bats fly from March to late October if the weather is hot and dry enough. Plan time to park and arrive at the bridge by sunset.

Let's talk about that smell. As you approach the Congress Avenue Bridge over Lady Bird Lake, a foul perfume slowly surrounds you. Congratulations! You've made it to the largest urban colony of Mexican free-tailed bats in the world. Why here? Renovations to the bridge in 1980 inadvertently created perfect lodges for these tiny migrating mammals. Stinkers though bats may be, these nocturnal beings are an iconic Austin attraction.

The bats fly here from warmer Mexican roosts in early spring, though rising Texas temperatures have some migrating as early as January or February. Male bats roost separately, but mother bats live under Congress Avenue Bridge in crevices. Each one will have one pup in June, who will learn to fly by late July, doubling the bat population that takes to the skies.

While our flying mammals are loved today, they were not always popular. In the 1980s, city officials proposed installing barricades under Congress Avenue Bridge when they noticed that the spot had become a regular place for bats to roost. Bat Conservation International stepped in to boost the local bat reputation, extoling their benefit as pest controllers. Did you know that bats can eat up to two-thirds their body weight in insects nightly? Collectively, that adds up to 100,000 to 300,000 pounds of moths, mosquitos, and crickets every night, which saves lots of valuable crops from obliteration.

To see the bats, timing is everything. There are no guarantees that the colony will fly out every night, but the sight is definitely worth repeat attempts should you miss a launch. About

Mexican free-tailed bats

People await the bats on and below Congress Avenue Bridge.

30 to 45 minutes before sundown is the usual time for nightly flights, but drought years might force the bats out up to an hour early. Hot, dry days in July and August make for the best bat viewing. Earlier in the spring works too, but the cool, damp weather means a late emergence. Mid-May to June are the worst times to catch a bat flight, because pregnant mother bats fly out later and are not as visible against the dark sky. The whole spectacle, from the first swirling groups of bats taking off to the last, can take up to an hour.

My favorite place to watch this natural phenomenon is atop the Congress Avenue Bridge itself. The northeast side offers the fullest views of the column of bats twirling up from underneath. This popular viewing area gets crowded, so arrive early to claim your spot at the railing. Alternatively, skip the crowds and head to the grassy hill along the Lady Bird Lake, below the Congress Avenue Bridge to the southeast. Viewers sit and relax here until showtime, usually not standing until the echolocating bats emerge. The hill is also a good spot for photos, because you'll capture people watching from the bridge in your frame. Access the grassy spot via the Ann and Roy Butler Hike-and-Bike Trail.

As a third option, you can take to the water. Rent a kayak or join a boat tour that will take you to the perfect spot. **Capital Cruises** (208 Barton Springs Rd., 512/480-9264, www. capitalcruises.com) and **Lone Star Riverboat** (208 Barton Springs Rd., 512/327-1388, https:// lonestarriverboat.com) both offer hour-long bat-watching tours. Boarding times change throughout the year and tickets tend to sell out a few weeks in advance, so book ahead online. Both boats board behind the Hyatt between the South First Street and South Congress Avenue.

The bats are not aggressive and don't harm the crowds. To help protect our flying friends, chiropterologists ask that you refrain from making loud noises or shining bright lights. If you find an injured bat, don't touch it and contact the Austin Bat Refuge immediately.

Today, bats are beloved Austin residents. After you've watched the overwhelming numbers of winged mammals smudge across the horizon, walk south from the bridge to Barton Springs Road and make a right. Cross the street to find a metal bat sculpture. *Nightwing* by Dale Whistler was installed in 1998, a symbol of the city's appreciation for the mammal Austin almost cleared out 15 years earlier. *Nightwing* rotates with the wind, a bat signal answered by millions of bats the city has grown to regard as a treasure.

Celebrate

A block party on Congress Avenue Bridge, **Bat Fest** (http://www.roadwayevents.com) brings live music, food trucks, and vendors together in celebration of our flying mammal friends. A surprisingly diverse musical lineup for the one-day, ticketed event features rap artists and rock bands. Bring the family during the day for kid-friendly activities or stay until midnight to enjoy the revelry; either way, be sure to stick around during sunset to see the celebrated bats take flight.

Connect with . . .

3 Go bar-hopping along Rainey Street

9 Kayak beautiful Lady Bird Lake

11 See why Austin is the "Live Music Capital of the World"

15 Check out the ever-changing South Congress Avenue

21 See the peacocks at Mayfield Park

Outdoor Adventures • Family Friendly

Why Go: See more than a dozen brilliantly plumed peacocks in an idyllic park in Austin.

Where: Mayfield Park • 3505 W 35th St. • https://mayfieldpark.org

Timing: Mayfield Park is open every day from 5am to 10pm and is free to the public. The weekdays are a few degrees quieter than the weekends.

Brilliant blue, shimmering green, and royal purple, Austin peacocks roam free. They drag their head-turning plumes behind them, ruffling feathers and hopping into trees. Without warning, a peacock can cross your path as you stroll through certain neighborhoods, unhurried as they glide past. To see an entire ostentation, or group of peacocks, for free, visit **Mayfield Park.**

▲ roosting peacock

This small west Austin park is home to nearly 20 of these beautiful birds, descendants of the peacocks that were gifted to the family who lived at the Mayfield-Gutsch Estate in 1935. That historic home still stands, and as the park grew up around it, the birds decided to stick close by. On most days, peacocks hang out just inside the park gates on either side of the short stone wall by the parking lot. Volunteers scatter seeds for them daily.

On my first visit, at least 15 dazzling fowl were eating seeds spread under the trees. More were up in the limbs above. "They live here," explained a friendly gardener when I ask how the peacocks were kept inside park bounds. "They kind of know this is their home, so they come back." During courting season, which usually starts in late winter and runs through spring, lucky visitors might get to see a peacock unfurl its gorgeous tail, showing off to peahens nearby. Most of the time, people will see the unbothered birds perch on stone gates, the Mayfield-Gutsch roof, or in the gardens.

peafowl

pond at Mayfield Park

a male peacock showing off his tailfeathers

On an average day, two or three human families loiter near the birds, trying to act non-threatening after reading the warning sign: "Peacocks are wild animals and may be aggressive during mating season." I've never seen a peacock lose its temper. On the other hand, I have heard a peacock scream. Always respect their space as you visit the peacocks at their home.

Don't miss the rest of the park while you're here. Twenty-three acres of nature preserve surround Mayfield Park, open to peacocks and hikers alike, with winding trails and snaking streams. Other wildlife includes blanket loafers and picnickers when the weather is nice. A few of the fancier visitors set up small tables with tablecloths, cheeses, and embroidered throw pillows to sit on, but wooden picnic tables are available to all outside the park gates under the shade of trees. Inside the stone walls, wooden benches are scattered around the park's community gardens. Sprouting buttercups and other flowers, 30 garden plots, lined in stones, bear little black nameplates and handwritten labels like "Wonderland" or "Sagan's Spot." Between the gardens and the old white house, six stone-lined ponds make the shape of a flower. Gardens float on the softly bubbling pond petals and koi swim inside.

Should one not be enough, Austin has a second location run by peacocks. In 2016, Austin residents in Bouldin Creek picked sides over complaints about pee-wits, the loud piercing screeches emitted by peafowl. Peacock lovers immediately posted signs in their yard that said "Peacocks welcome here" and "Save the peacocks" in a show of solidarity with the birds. If you want the peacock, you take the pee-wits. Bouldin Creek peacocks come from **Mattie's** (811 W Live Oak St., 512/444-1888, https://mattiesaustin.com), a historic home in the neighborhood that was converted to a Southern-style restaurant in 1946. The establishment has been known to host famous writers and celebrities, but the best known locally may be the fancy-feathered birds, who have called Mattie's home since the 1960s. An all-white peacock, like a wintery bird king, is known to roam from Mattie's and into the surrounding neighborhoods. Male peacocks need colorful plumes to attract females, so the white bird is on his own, but he is certainly well-loved by the community. I met him one summer as I walked to work. He gracefully strutted past, carefully evading a photo. The easiest way to see the white bird and his brilliant bird friends at Mattie's is to eat at the restaurant, which has ample grounds and impressive interior design.

Non-native to Texas, Austin peacocks share their space like good neighbors. The living jewels are loyal to the land and the hand that feeds them, never straying too far. They hop and peck with a glorious train like chickens of paradise, usually ignoring you unless you're seated on the ground with food. Beware. These usually docile animals are still wild creatures, like the rest of the population keeping Austin weird.

Connect with . . .

1 Howl at the moon in Zilker Park

15 Check out the ever-changing South Congress Avenue

24 Touch the sky at Mount Bonnell

22 **Walk among wildflowers**

Outdoor Adventures • Family Friendly • Best in Spring

Why Go: This collection of native Texas flowers, plants, and trees sprawling over 284 acres in southwest Austin offers a serene getaway for old and young, with playgrounds for kids across blooming landscapes and placid pathways.

Where: Lady Bird Johnson Wildflower Center • 4801 La Crosse Ave. • 512/232-0100 • www.wildflower.org

Timing: Keep a steady pace and you can cover the grounds in a little over an hour and a half, but plan for more time to stop and smell the roses (or to let the kids play at the playground). Sunny weekend days draw the community in, but weekdays are tranquil. Stop by as early as 9am and stay until 5pm or 8pm, depending on the day and the season. Hours vary with the sunset, so call ahead to be sure about closing times.

Past the entrance kiosk and at the end of the long stone walkway, a young, downy great horned owl gazed down from beside a rough-edged sotol plant. The baby owl held the gaze of a few

▲ Lady Bird Johnson Wildflower Center

transfixed families. A woman standing nearby taking photos explained that it was a fledgling, and the owl should drop to the ground and hop around eventually. Athena, its mother, had nested in this corner perch of the Lady Bird Johnson Wildflower Center for at least a decade. Species like the owl are comfortable among the native plants here. Preserving the symbiotic relationship between native wildlife and native landscapes is the goal of the Wildflower Center.

Texas plants are celebrated here, where wildflowers, grasses, shrubs, and trees are carefully cultivated. Three miles of tended trails weave through central gardens featuring neatly labeled plants, butterfly gardens, savannahs, and an arboretum. Playgrounds for kids and benches for adults dot the 284-acre campus, making this a peaceful escape for the whole family. Admission is $12 for adults, with tiers of prices for children of different ages, seniors, and military. Parking is free and easy to navigate.

Prairie verbena at Lady Bird Johnson Wildflower Center

young great horned owl

the Theme Gardens and JJ Priour sculpture

The center is beautiful year-round. Springtime is a great bet for seeing blooms and animals. Summertime flowers include the vibrant rock rose, orange Texas lantana, and purple bluebell wildflowers. In fall, colors turn shades of blazing sunset in plants like the Virginia creeper and the Gulf muhly. Celebrate trees during the Winter Tree Fest, where you can climb the trunks in the arboretum.

Designated as the official Botanic Garden and Arboretum of Texas in 2017, the Center was founded in 1982 and was originally located in East Austin. Now located about 11 miles south of downtown, the Wildflower Center has grown from that 60-acre site to this bigger campus. You'll enter through a large courtyard and walk down past the café to the **Theme Gardens.** If you can only visit one area, make it this one. The 23 stone-lined beds each come with their own theme, like the Salvia Garden (featuring big red sage) and the Healing Garden (with gayfeather and parsley hawthorn). The Fiber and Dye Garden has burgundy winecup and golden groundsel, while the Hummingbird Garden has red yucca. The Pollinator Habitat Garden, complete with a small pond, grows plants to support butterflies and insects.

▲ view from the center

Tucked away on the northeast side of the Theme Gardens, the 16-acre **Mollie Steves Zachry Texas Arboretum** is surprisingly easy to miss, but once you're there you'll see the oak tree collection and the "Cathedral of Swings," a collection of wooden swings hanging from an old oak tree for people of all ages to enjoy. The Hall of Texas Heroes is a plot of oaks propagated from some of Texas' oldest and most famous trees, including a Wedding Oak once used by Indigenous people to marry under.

Regular **events** are a great reason to visit. Throughout the year, Twilight Tuesdays offer live music until 8pm, with some Canine Nights where dogs are allowed. Yoga classes with singing bowls are a recurring Sunday event, with parent and toddler yoga classes held every Tuesday. Weekly story time for kids in the morning might also interest families with youngsters. In December, don't miss Luminations, when you can visit after dark and see the center lit up with thousands of luminaries. The lighting installations make the space a bit more magical.

Keep an eye out for the little lizards, shimmering blue beetles, and snakes. "We share this space with rattlesnakes," proclaim signs throughout the gardens, but never fear—snakes are a good thing. It means that the habitat is healthy. Stay on the path and you'll be fine.

Connect with . . .

5 Taste Texas at addictive barbecue joints

14 Eat like royalty at food trucks

18 Hike the Greenbelt

23 **Bask in the glow of holiday lights**

Family Friendly • Best in Winter

Why Go: These festive, family-friendly displays are all beautiful, bright, and wheel-chair accessible, making them the perfect way for the whole family to get immersed in the holiday spirit.

Where: You can see lights in Austin at Mozart's Coffee Roasters on Lady Bird Lake; or venture 20 miles northwest of Austin to Lakeway or 30 miles north to Georgetown.

Timing: Holiday lights go up in late November and last until early January. Plan an hour to bask in the glow of the lights at Georgetown and Mozart's, and around half an hour for the Lakeway trail.

There is not a lot of snow in Austin, but in the spirit of dressing for the holiday you want, the city and surrounding communities offer up more than a few dazzling light displays to enjoy as the mild Texas winter sets in.

One of Austin's loveliest displays comes from local coffee roaster and palace of sumptuous pastries, **Mozart's Coffee Roasters** (3825 Lake Austin Blvd., 512/477-2900, https://mozartscoffee.com), which has put on their annual Christmas event since 2010. Sitting on the shore of Lady Bird Lake, the shop is in one of the most beautiful locations in Austin, boasting stunning views of the water from its spacious upper and lower decks. Even with only a few stringed lights, the setting alone with would be hard to resist, but the transformation into a musical lightshow makes this a great bet for a family outing.

Santa's Sleigh outside the shop in red and green lights is popular for families to sit in and take photos with. Bordering the entire shop are 25 white, blue, and violet cloth roses with garlands of icicle lights strung beneath. On the deck, a grand piano sparkles in lights from a stage where a pianist plays live holiday music as behind him shines a wall of nutcrackers, longhorns, and snowflakes in time with the music. Giant gift boxes hang from the big tree on the deck, and cinnamon-sugar pretzels and hot cocoa with marshmallows are available for anyone with a

1: picnicking under the lights at Georgetown
2: Georgetown holiday lights **3:** light show at
Mozart's **4:** silk flowers at Mozart's

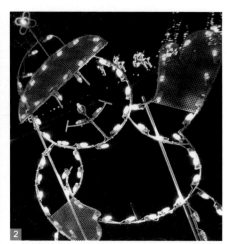

1: Lakeway's lights **2:** snowman at Lakeway's Trail of Lights **3:** Christmas tree of lights **4:** having fun at Lakeway's Trail of Lights

sweet tooth. Advance tickets for a seated or standing table are required for the one-hour event. They are less than $10 per table, and easy to reserve online.

Friends and I were at the **Trail of Lights** (1102 Lohmans Crossing Rd., Lakeway, 512/261-1010, www.lakeway-tx.gov) in Lakeway when a toddler in a red puffy jacket ran down the path squealing with delight, arms outstretched to embrace the colorful scene. "The best part of these lights is watching your kids get excited about it," said a person on the trail. My friends and I don't have kids, but seeing other people ecstatically take in the bright lights was the highlight of our trip out to the small community west of Austin. For a tiny person, the lights are especially enchanting.

This small, free trail was open from 6pm to midnight, no reservations were required, but unwrapped toy donations were accepted and encouraged. My friends and I made it through the trail in half an hour, during which time we took photos with our faces in the tinseled bear cutouts, and we tried to remember the lyrics to "The Twelve Days of Christmas," which we suspected was the theme of the numbered lights display. We did our best to snap a photo of the brilliant tunnel of lights flashing in sync with music playing from a small speaker while it was completely lit up, and we noticed that more than a few families waited very patiently for us to get the shot we wanted.

Twenty-five miles north of Austin, the city of Georgetown lights up their historic downtown every year from mid-November to early January. The free display, called the **Lighting of the Square** (710 S Main St., Georgetown, 512/943-1100, https://visit.georgetown.org), uses thousands of white string lights to illuminate the Beaux-Arts style Williamson County Courthouse and the surrounding Victorian-style shops. Families spread blankets out on the courthouse lawn and bask in the glow of two huge green trees of lights. Public art from local artists on every corner showcases an abundance of creativity here, like Linda Wilde's *The Optimist* on the corner of Main and 7th Streets which features a blue jewel-toned mosaic duck. Each evening, restaurants and shops around the square offer their best ice cream sandwiches, local wines, and cold brews. Standing beneath the big red bows on the Georgetown streetlamps with not a speck of snow in sight was a perfect Texas Christmas.

24 Touch the sky at Mount Bonnell

Outdoor Adventures • Only in Austin

Why Go: Two of Austin's most famous overlooks offer the best views of rolling limestone hills and the Colorado River winding through west Austin.

Where: Pennybacker Bridge (also called Austin 360 Bridge, 5300 N Capital of Texas Hwy.); Covert Park at Mount Bonnell (3800 Mt. Bonnell Rd., 512/974-6700, https://mountbonnell.com)

Timing: Head out to the Pennybacker Bridge Overlook for a singular view of the Colorado River and the iconic Pennybacker Bridge, then drive 10 minutes to the much-loved Mount Bonnell viewpoint. You can reasonably visit both in an hour. Sunrise and sunset are spectacular at either spot.

There's something stunning about the **Pennybacker Bridge.** You come across it in West Austin as you cruise Highway 360, something of a scenic thoroughfare in itself, with nary a billboard in sight. A 1,150-foot-long, 600-foot-wide suspension bridge over the Colorado River completed in 1982, the Pennybacker feels like a modern art sculpture. Above is blue sky, below is river, and framing each side are the long limestone cliffs and shrubby trees of the Balcones escarpment, the fault line that created the Hill Country's famously rolling landscape. The first time you cross, you'll want to slow down time or turn the car around and cross another half dozen times to enjoy the view. But the view from afar is the real destination. People cram their automobiles along the side of the road to hike up an overlooking cliff face and take in the view with family and friends. Named for engineer Percy V. Pennybacker, the bridge over Highway 360 has no support columns underneath, which makes it especially impressive to admire from a distance. The view from the overlook is so stunning, it's almost a mandatory stop.

To get to the **Pennybacker Bridge Overlook,** head to the north side of the bridge, pull over to the west side of the road, and park on the dirt shoulder near the other cars. The trail starts at about the midway point of the strip of parking along the shoulder, closest to the west leg of the bridge. Lock your car and always hide any valuables, then look for the white dirt

Pennybacker Bridge

view from the Pennybacker Bridge Overlook

path leading to a short 0.1-mile rocky climb to the top of this piece of the Balcones escarpment. Spanish colonialists thought the rock faces of this escarpment looked like balconies...hence, the name. There are no handrails and the rocks are worn from use, so step carefully, and try to wear shoes with tread. Soak in the views from the summit before hiking back down.

For another tried-and-true viewpoint, make the ten-minute (roughly five-mile) drive to Mount Bonnell. Drive north on Highway 360 (the road Pennybacker Bridge is on) and, in less than half a mile, turn right onto Ranch to Market 2222. In about two miles, turn right onto Mt. Bonnell Road. Follow for another two miles until you see the free parking on your right. The drive follows the Colorado River, and for a stretch of 2222, you'll see a cliff wall rising up on one side while on the other, the land drops away for stunning views of the river. Mt. Bonnell Road is smaller, winding, and lushly tree-lined.

At 775 feet, **Mount Bonnell** is known as the highest point in Austin and is another great place to snap photos with the Colorado River behind you. The views from Pennybacker and Mount Bonnell are similar, but both places are local favorites—and Mount Bonnell has the add-

▲ view from Mount Bonnell

ed bonus of the Austin skyline in its vistas. A short (0.3 mile) but rocky and steep staircase leads to a scenic overlook. There's a handrail here for extra self-hoisting power, and your huffing and puffing will be rewarded with some of the best views in Austin. From this perch above the fancy mansions and boat docks, you'll see a vast stretch of natural beauty, with Pennybacker Bridge off in the distance to the west. Picnic tables makes this a great place to enjoy a snack and soak in the sights.

This area has a long history of legends, including one about a woman named Antoinette leaping to her death from Mount Bonnell after learning that her fiancé had been killed. Another says that couples who make the climb together will fall in love. Sam Houston is said to have called Mount Bonnell the place the devil used to tempt Jesus with the riches of the land.

Although the area is technically called Covert Park, locals refer to it as Mount Bonnell. Whatever you call it, one look at those views and you'll know why this has been a popular tourist destination since the 1850s.

Connect with . . .
21 See the peacocks at Mayfield Park

25 Hunt for murals

Art & Culture • Only in Austin

Why Go: Austin is an artistic treasure hunt. Everything from beloved 1970s murals to more contemporary art makes the city's very walls vibrant destinations.

Where: Art can be found throughout the city. There's a particularly high concentration on Cesar Chavez Street, east of Interstate 35, and on South Lamar Boulevard, between 3rd and 5th Streets.

Timing: The traditional way to experience murals is by accidentally stumbling upon them, but if you're determined to see them all, hop in the car and make a day of it.

Street art in Austin has grown over the years—from illegal to accepted and even encouraged. Today, the values, character, and history of the city breathe through the art on its walls.

Austin's reputation for murals began in 2011 with the **Hope Outdoor Gallery** (www.hopeoutdoorgallery.com), a hub for muralists and graffiti artists like Sloke One, Erik Ross, and Skele, who have created incredible pieces on the walls of empty buildings for over a decade. Today, the original location of the gallery lies abandoned, but it's scheduled to reopen in 2021 as an open-air art park on Dalton Lane near the Austin-Bergstrom Airport.

Some of Austin's murals are so well-known, they're commemorated in souvenirs—like Daniel Johnston's iconic **"Hi, How are you?"** (2100 Guadalupe Ave.), featuring a black and white frog with a kind expression. The affectionate **"I love you so much"** mural at Jo's Coffee (1300 S Congress Ave.) has inspired spoofs in the same style around the city: **"Jesus loves you so much"** (E Monroe St., a few blocks east of Home Slice Pizza), **"I hate you so much"** (Bungalow, 92 Rainey St.), and **"wash your hands"** (Barton Springs Saloon, 424 S Lamar Blvd.). The highly Instagrammable **"Greetings from Austin"** (1720 S 1st St.), by Todd Sanders and Rory Skagen, looks like a vintage postcard.

Cesar Chavez Street, to the east of Interstate 35, is a hotspot for murals. Queer bilingual Latin folk singer-songwriter **Gina Chavez** (2400 E Cesar Chavez St.) is immortalized by Levi Ponce in greyscale between Chalmers Avenue and Chicon Street. On the same wall, the elegant,

1: *Be Well* section by Uloang **2:** *Be Well* section by Rex Hamilton **3:** *Be Well* section by Carmen Rangel **4:** *Be Well* section by Niz

mirrored **"Grey Ghost"** is a portrait of blues legend Roosevelt Williams by The Mosaic Workshop, created with a grant from the City of Austin Cultural Arts Department. Three blocks east, on the corner of Robert T. Martinez Jr. Street, you'll find the benevolent vintage Godzilla monster **"Hola Friend"** by Will Hatch Crosby, a tribute to Daniel Johnston. To get a taste of mosaic artist Stefanie Distefano's many pieces, check out **"The Virgin"** and **"The Ghandi,"** next to each other on the corner of Chicon Street and Cesar Chavez Street.

To encourage self-care during the pandemic in 2020, six artists gave the Lamar Underpass a makeover. Raasin McIntosh of Raasin the Sun, the non-profit that helped curate these murals, titled the collection of murals ***Be Well,*** saying "We do this to unite people, to inspire, and to make communities resilient." Find the 10,000-square-foot tribute to the embattled-but-creative spirit of the times on South Lamar Boulevard, between 3rd and 5th Streets.

Luis Angulo, known as Uloang, painted men and women siloed from one another by thick, colorful rectangles, layered like bolts of fabric. Some stare at their phones, some strain to see one another. Kimie Flores painted forlorn figures—face in palms, a hole through the chest with

▲ part of the *Be Well* mural by artist Kimie Flores

122

a floating star, a boy holding a worried flower—to remind us that "we are more than the set of limitations we are forced to accept." A long white snake in patches of blue scales swims through Carmen Rangel's work. Rex Hamilton's color palette vibrates, featuring serene women clutching sunflowers or basking in the sun. Samara Banks painted Black bodies in gentle repose to encourage rest as a form of resistance. Eleanor Herasimchuk, known as Niz, painted women as butterflies with eyes downcast in prayer. Around the south corner, Sadé Lawson painted three women among lotus flowers to encourage the embrace of emotions often considered "weak." Throughout the collection, phrases like "it's okay not to be okay" and "rest is necessary" reiterate how the murals encourage mental health.

Some other noteworthy murals are spread across town. Roots rock star **Doug Sahm** (Nickel City, 11th St. and Lydia St.) is memorialized by stencil artist Federico Archuleta, also known as El Federico. Other pieces include **"JohnnyCash"** (24th St. and Guadalupe St.), **"Virgin de Guadalupe"** (Tesoros Trading Company, 1500 S Congress Ave.), and **"til death do us part"** (7th St. and Waller St.). Niz painted a tribute to **Angela Davis** outside of Home Slice Pizza (1415 S Congress Ave.) in response to the Black Lives Matter movement. Native Hostel (807 E 4th St.), off of Interstate 35 northbound, features a mural by Chris Rogers memorializing **George Floyd.**

Public art flourishes in part thanks to Austin's Art in Public Spaces program, which has contributed to over 300 works of art since 1985. But it's thanks to the legacy of the artists themselves that Austin is covered in art today.

Connect with . . .

- ⑩ Run with the cool crowd on East 6th Street
- ⑬ Dive into Latin American art at Blanton Museum
- ⑮ Check out the ever-changing South Congress Avenue
- ⑯ See cutting-edge art at Austin's East Side galleries

26 Unwrap an ice-cold *paleta*

Taste of Texas • Only in San Antonio • Family Friendly

Why Go: Taste the refreshing, fruity frozen treat that's an authentic piece of Latinx childhood, perfect on a hot summer day.

Where: El Paraiso Ice Cream (1934 Fredericksburg Rd., San Antonio, 210/737-8101, www.elparaisoicecream.com), Paleteria (510 S Alamo St., Suite 104, San Antonio, 210/954-6753)

Timing: El Paraiso is open every day except a few major holidays. Drop by in the afternoon or evening, especially on a hot day. Paleteria is open Thursday-Sunday.

Children from Chicano neighborhoods remember the *paleta*-man pushing his pale green cart down the street, tapping the row of bells on the handle, and selling delicious frozen treats on hot summer days. At the time, you couldn't find *paletas* in the freezer with other ice creams at American grocery stores. When he nodded and handed you your favorite flavor, a little thrill ran through your greedy fingers, even if it was simple, boring banana. Then you sucked the flavor in until the ice got pale.

Paletas are Mexican popsicles, essentially. But classic American popsicles taste like re-incarnated candy, if they are fruit-flavored at all. Classic *paletas* are made of actual fruit and juice, sweet because of natural sugars and sometimes creamy and rich with the addition of milk. Traditional flavors are mango, coconut, strawberry, watermelon, and cantaloupe, but there are also savory and sour options like tamarind and soursop.

San Antonio's **El Paraiso Ice Cream** is the best known *paleta*-dealer in the city. Tell the locals that you plan to cruise by the shop and they invariably comment "Oh, you're going to the OG location," by which they mean that this shop has been around for a long time. Established in 1984, El Paraiso still sells *paletas* at just fifty cents each.

Nowadays, brick and mortar *paleta* shops have become fixtures in the community. El Paraiso is housed in a small building with an arched roof painted in blue and white stripes.

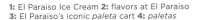

1: El Paraiso Ice Cream **2:** flavors at El Paraiso
3: El Paraiso's iconic *paleta* cart **4:** *paletas*

▲ display case at Paleteria

▲ Paleteria menu

They offer 24 flavors: 12 fruit-based bars and 12 milk-based bars. *Mango chile* and *piña chile* are perfect people who enjoy chili powder sprinkled on fruit, typical in Mexico.

I've never had a pickle *paleta,* but I decided to try one on my first visit to El Paraiso, where the flavor was listed, unassumingly, halfway down the list of fruit-based popsicle bars, between the mango and cantaloupe. I asked the attendant what second flavor would balance pickle out and he recommended cheesecake. Good advice. I left with flavors that may seem like a strange combination but are often paired on fancy cheese boards.

Now that *paletas* have finally made their way onto the shelves of American grocery stores, a new kind of *paleta* has emerged. Dipped in chocolate, and coated in coconut flakes, sprinkles, cracker crumbs, or gummy bears, this *paleta* is flamboyant and a little decadent, the superlative of the plain frozen popsicle. You can try it at **Paleteria** downtown. The flavors rotate often. You can still get the tried-and-true fruit flavors (with real chunks of fruit) like strawberry and coconut, or even guava-pineapple, as well as more unusual options, such as Mexican candy flavors like *mazapan* (honey and almond meal) and American milk-bars like Fruity Pebbles and Pumpkin Pie for the holidays. The creativity of the toppings here sparks conversation with friends. I overheard a couple discuss the best way to present the Fruity Pebbles popsicle, deciding that serving it in a small cardboard cereal box, with a pop made of just the milk soaked in the cereal and Fruity Pebble crunch topping sprinkled on top would be the ultimate.

How do you order your *paleta*? The classic, naked *paleta* on a wooden stick with little chunks of fruit inside may be the best place to start. Or gravitate to your favorite flavor and then try something completely out of left field for your palette if you are so inclined. Push the boundaries and dress it up with crunchy candy toppings or syrupy drizzle. Whatever you choose, don't forget to say *"muchas gracias"* to your local *paletero* or *paletera*.

Connect with . . .

28 Eat tacos for all three meals
32 Shop in "Little Mexico" at San Antonio's Historic Market Square
35 Stroll through King William Historic District

27 Immerse yourself in art at Hopscotch

Art & Culture

Why Go: Leave the mundane behind at the most breathtaking immersive art experience in Texas.

Where: Hopscotch • 711 Navarro, Suite 100, San Antonio • https://letshopscotch.com

Timing: Skip into Hopscotch Friday through Sunday. Hours vary, so be sure to reserve tickets in advance to guarantee entry at your preferred time. All ages are welcome until 7pm, after which Hopscotch is 18 and up only. Plan to spend an hour playing and snapping photos inside the exhibit.

Passive viewing is out. For most of the installations at Hopscotch, your participation makes the art work. The work inside is a sugar-rush of eye-candy that encourages the kind of light-hearted movement and joy the name Hopscotch evokes. Across 20,000 square feet in downtown San Antonio, the two-story collection of interactive and immersive rooms are mostly large-scale, technology-driven playgrounds of work by artists from Austin—where Hopscotch debuted—and San Antonio but also from as far as Moscow and Barcelona.

While day-of online tickets are possible, reserve one day ahead of time to secure your preferred entry time and to save some money. Entry times are scheduled every 15 minutes, but you'll want to arrive early to linger at the ground-floor bar out front. The Hopscotch lounge pours specialty cocktails like the Rabbit-Hole Rita made with local Dessert Door sotol, agave, and lime juice, as well as mocktails, cold brew, and more. Take your drink with you into the gallery or enjoy it on the sunny patio out front, where rotating food trucks cycle through on a bi-monthly basis. Take in large murals, floor-to-ceiling windows covered in black lace, and Ilya Tinker's ***Down the Rabbit Hole,*** a leaping rabbit sculpture made of small, holographic triangles suspended above a stairwell as you make your way from the lounge to the lobby. Attendants encourage you to "tag us in your photos" as you walk through.

On my first visit with friends, two rooms stole the show for me. Less was more in my favorite exhibit, ***Color Therapy,*** from Austin artist Polis. Viewers are wrapped by a continuous,

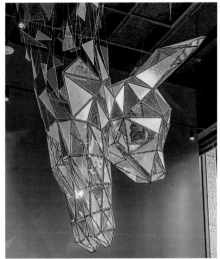

▲ *Down the Rabbit Hole* by Ilya Tinker

▲ Hopscotch!

Color Therapy by Polis

circular screen illuminated blue, violet, green, pink, and red, with the aim of balancing energy centers through color therapy. In the other room, LA artist Matt Elson constructed the most surreal art in Hopscotch. **Infinity Boxes** is a series of small boxes you peer into to find yourself transformed into something like a carousel of coin-operated fortune tellers. These eye-level reflections were like magnets for curious viewers. My friends and I looked inside one box and strobing lights appeared to merge our reflections in a psychedelic hallucination.

For the art-should-make-you-think crowd, **Rainbow Cave** from Brooklyn artist Basia Goszczynska is a cavern of thousands of scrunched up white plastic shopping bags installed from floor to ceiling. Illuminated by soft cool light, the installation of an artificial "natural" space was simultaneously beautiful and uncomfortable. The sense of being physically overwhelmed with just a small portion of what is a huge amount of refuse generated daily was enough to make me pause. And were these bags even clean? And is the urge for sterility a part of the problem?

Secrets by Wide Awake Creative is a modern-day confessional with the aim of catharsis.

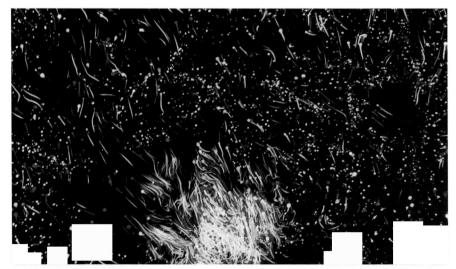

▲ part of *Symbiosis* by Kuflex

A blurb on the wall explains that kept secrets increase anxiety and loneliness, and that the act of sharing a secret can create feelings of relief. Old school phone booths on the wall dispensed the anonymous secrets from other Hopscotch visitors at the push of an orange button. The secrets were recorded in two small rooms earlier that month, an attendant assured. She added that processing the secrets took weeks, so we could leave our own and not worry about our friends hearing them anytime soon. Visitors could even call in later and leave secrets on an answering machine if they wanted to. "Do you have anything to hide?" asked one friend.

Russian artist Kuflex created **Symbiosis,** which features interactive video projections in two separate rooms where visitors' movements elicit slow, precise color-soaked screen reflections. On one screen, your movement is reflected back to you in symmetrical forms inspired by exotic insects and extraterrestrial forms, and on the other, your movement takes the form of sweeping rushes of light and color. Barcelona's Playmodes created **VJ Yourself,** a kaleidoscope where the viewer takes the role of the crystals in view. Minimal house and techno plays while the viewer is reflected across a large mirror dozens of times over, fanned and reshuffled like a deck of cards.

Permanently housed in San Antonio, Hopscotch has room to grow into something potentially as saturated as Meow Wolf's original space in Santa Fe. Even in its current form, Hopscotch is already a landmark destination for lovers of visual arts.

Connect with . . .

36 Take in art along the River Walk

28 Eat tacos for all three meals

Taste of Texas • Only in San Antonio

Why Go: In San Antonio, there are tacos for every mood, every eater, and every time of day. Spend a day falling in love with the traditional flavors of Mexican and Tex-Mex cuisine.

Where: Citywide

Timing: Hours vary from place to place, with some focusing on breakfast and lunch, while others cater to dinner and the late-night crowd.

One day it hit me: some people in the United States don't know about breakfast tacos. Not only that, but some might hear the word "taco" and imagine dry, crispy shells filled with ground beef and shredded iceberg lettuce. God blessed Texas, as the saying goes, and we have show-stopping tacos here for breakfast, lunch, and dinner.

There is a joke in Austin that says for good tacos you should get on IH-35, head south, and keep on driving until you get to San Antonio, and that's for good reason. Mexican cuisine is recognized by UNESCO as a cultural heritage, and the Latinx population here is huge. Ask around and you'll hear people agree on a few of the best places to stop. If you're adventurous, you should pick a few taco-filling anchors (for example, *al pastor* and *barbacoa*) and try to sample them at a few taquerias. Tacos are part of a long history and traditions run deep, but personally I'm a fan of creativity. A great taco is a great taco.

Austin claims credit for introducing breakfast tacos to the world, a dubious assertion that triggered a guffaw heard around the state, especially in San Antonio. Regardless of where they originated, breakfast tacos are now considered Tex-Mex canon, with roots on both sides of the border. At **Con Huevos Tacos** (1629 E Houston St., 210/229-9295, www.conhuevostacos. com), the tortillas, corn and flour alike, are homemade. Try the flour for breakfast and you'll be served a tortilla as big as your face. For breakfast tacos, order the Irma, eggs scrambled in *salsa verde* with Oaxacan cheese, cilantro, and thick avocado slices. The Carmen, with potato, egg,

Taquitos West Ave.

taco plate at Taquitos West Ave.

and cheese, is another satisfying meal and large enough for a person who normally orders two tacos. Add bacon or chorizo to satisfy a meat craving, and don't skip the salsa.

For lunch, try a Tex-Mex adaptation and San Antonio favorite: the puffy taco. Made of masa and freshly fried into a shell shape, puffies are crunchy on the outside and moist on the inside. Since 1978, family-owned **Henry's Puffy Tacos** (6030 Bandera Rd., 210/647-8339, www.henryspuffytacos.com) has served the best. The shredded chicken is divine, though beef and beans are also available. Topped with lettuce, tomato, and cheese, these tacos bring people together. Upon reuniting with long lost family of my own in San Antonio, we decided to drive across town to Henry's, and every single person of our very large party ordered puffies. The puffy taco is also the official mascot of the San Antonio Missions, a little league baseball team.

Taquitos West Ave. (2818 West Ave., 210/525-9888) has long lines out the door and through the parking lot, even late on a Sunday night. The lights are bright, the food is fresh, and the steam rises in billowing clouds behind the counter. A plate of five tacos with fresh raw onions, cilantro, and thick slices of cucumber comes in at under $10, and you can mix and match

▲ Tacos El Regio St. Mary's

fillings. The *al pastor* (pork) is excellent, as is the *bistec* (beef), but the *suadero* is from another planet. Popular in Mexico, the fatty and sweet *suadero* is from the cow's belly, marinated in orange and lime juice before being cooked, chopped, shredded, and browned. The resulting flavor is richer than Jeff Bezos, and perfect with a hit of the acidic *salsa verde* or *roja* served that comes with each plate.

Still hungry? The mini tacos at **Tacos El Regio St. Mary's** (2726 N St. Mary's St., 210/782-2272, https://tacos-el-regio-mexican-restaurant.business.site) reign supreme. You'll find this place in a plain yellow trailer on St. Mary's Street, a popular strip of nightlife in the Alamo city. Four minis with thick slices of lime, avocado, lots of crumbled cheese, cilantro, and fresh onions are $8. My friends swear by the bean and cheese, but for me the all-star was the *al pastor* taco. Second place went to the fajita chicken, which many places neglect, but it was seasoned to perfection at El Regio. Stop in after you've been at the local bars for a late-night pick-me-up to eat standing in the parking lot with your friends.

Connect with . . .

㉖ Unwrap an ice-cold *paleta*

29 Get spooked on a ghost tour

Family Friendly

Why Go: Hundred-year-old ghosts chill the blood at famous, haunted San Antonio landmarks. Try to spot an apparition on a walking tour through downtown as you learn the fascinating, tragic life stories behind the spirits that refuse to transition.

Where: Sister's Grimm Ghost Tours • 204 Alamo Plaza • 210/638-1338 • www.sisters-grimmghosttour.com

Timing: Daily walking tours begin at 8:30pm and are 90 minutes long.

The Sister's Grimm Haunted History walking tour feels eerie before it begins. Find the front of the Menger Hotel. The first story is awash in light from bright globes on the Victorian streetlamps outside. Above you, striped green and white awnings cast shadows over the double doors and windows overlooking Alamo Plaza. On the third story, over intricate iron balconies, the light is dimmest, though none of that matters, because you are headed down the alleyway on the right.

When you reach the end of the alley, you'll find people milling around on the steps of the Sister's Grimm shop waiting for the rest of the tour group to arrive. On my first visit, I was gently rattled when the guide checked me in and then forgot who I was 15 minutes later. He asked to check me in a second time. Worse, I had forgotten him and was confused as to whether he was the same man from earlier or if I was already in a kind of off-menu supernatural occurrence.

Prepare to hear, or maybe be a part of, a few scary ghost stories. Along the way, you'll be joined by 5-34 living souls. This mile-and-a-half leisurely ramble through downtown San Antonio is a spooky way to spend $20 ($15 for ages 6-12). Wear comfortable shoes; wheelchairs of course are also welcome. Book your tickets online ahead of time to guarantee your ghoulish evening. Sister's Grim also offers a two-and-a-half-hour bus tour ($40) to many of the same sites as the walking tour, with extra stops in San Antonio's Old Red Light District and historic

▲ Casino Club

▲ the old Bexar County Jail

▲ San Fernando Cathedral

cemetery. To dine among the spirits in the Menger, Sister's Grimm will arrange a three-course dinner in the Victorian-era Colonial Room inside the hotel ($75).

Our first stop was the **Menger Hotel.** Built in 1859, it claims to be the oldest continually operating hotel this side of the Mississippi and is rumored to have 36 known shades, or ghosts, inside. Theodore Roosevelt recruited men here for his volunteer army of Rough Riders, and bar patrons still see the 26th American President asking strangers to sign on for his volunteer calvary. Other well-known spirits include Captain Richard King of King Ranch and Sally White, a loyal chambermaid shot to death by her jealous husband.

The tour moved to **The Alamo,** where hooded figures brandishing flaming swords were said to have played a major role in preserving the Spanish mission. After Mexican General Santa Ana defeated men fighting for Texan independence, lore has him sending his men to destroy the Mission lest the structure become a uniting symbol for Texans. When the men arrived at the old Misión San Antonio de Valero, ethereal figures protected the grounds. Those blazing angels still appear to guests peering from hotel rooms at the Alamo today. Nearby the **Emily**

▲ The Alamo

Morgan Hotel, named after the famous *Yellow Rose of Texas* song, is a former hospital with a crematorium in the basement that is rumored to still smell of the decay on certain floors.

Other stops include the **Casino Club,** an old German social club turned residential building where a young boy once took a photo of a ghost in the glass doors; the **San Fernando Cathedral** where a spectral stallion serves as a reminder of the short-lived truce between settlers and Lipan Apaches who literally buried hatchets and a white horse as a peace treaty; and the **Spanish Governor's Palace,** where the Lady in Grey can be seen looking out of the window.

The last stop at the old **Bexar County Jail** is a goosebumps-inducing finale. With reports of guests and workers who hallucinated bodies seeming to drop from above, felt freezing cold rooms, and heard inexplicable voices, this stop was the most hair-raising.

According to our guide, chimeras sometimes appear in photos, especially if the photographer plays with the settings and makes black and white or sepia-toned copies to inspect. He encouraged everyone to take turns snapping a few pictures at the glass doors and windows. "Let me know if you think you have something and I'll take a look," he said, insisting that apparitions were more than creepy reflections. He'd seen more than a few people rattled about what they saw in their cameras later. But a ghost would say that kind of thing.

Connect with . . .

28 Eat tacos for all three meals

30 Wear a flower crown at Fiesta

Only in San Antonio • Art & Culture • Family Friendly

Why Go: San Antonio puts on its most colorful coat for more than a week of spectacular float parades, music, and events during Fiesta. Experience a Mexican rodeo or just people-watch in the festive metropolis.

Where: Downtown San Antonio (fiestasanantonio.org)

Timing: Fiesta takes place over 11 days in April but you can easily sample all the festival has to offer in one day. Go early to catch a parade and stay through the afternoon to graze on foods from the many food vendors, have a margarita, and enjoy the music and people-watching.

San Antonio's Fiesta began 130 years ago as a war reenactment but with flowers, where participants pelted each other with bouquets instead of bullets. Over the years, the annual event morphed into a parade and a tradition was born. Today, Fiesta is a party in downtown San Antonio, spilling across the city for 11 days. The seminal Battle of Flowers parade honoring fighters at the battles of Alamo and Goliad—when the state sought independence from Mexico—is now one of many parades. Visitors crowd the sidewalks each spring, sipping Micheladas, walking along the river as illuminated boat-floats drift by. Mariachis serenade and *folklorico* performers dazzle with elaborate dresses and *zapateado,* or stamping feet. Take in the revelry and family-friendly fun, not to mention the killer food.

The April events kick off with the stunning Battle of Flowers Parade, then sees the splashy Texas Cavaliers River Parade send floats down the River Walk, and ends with the illumed Fiesta Flambeau Parade 11 days later. Colorful cultural events in between celebrate Mexican and Texan heritage. Block partiers collect hundreds of commemorative medals tossed like Mardi Gras beads from "royalty" on floats, wear delicate flower crowns, and bask in the lively outdoor party for all ages. Confetti from painted egg shells, *cascarones,* litter the streets. Chili contests, fireworks, bike rides, and more are all part of the festivities. There are also tons of food vendors selling treats, like my favorites: *tamales, churros,* and *aguas frescas.* A few vendors will only

1: *escaramuza* **2:** a *charro* doing a rope trick
3: colorful *cascarones* **4:** flower crowns in the
crowd

accept cash, so come prepared to pay in paper for a few things, and wear comfortable shoes to explore the city around the thousands who visit for Fiesta every year.

Of all the events to choose from, Mexico's national sport might be the most transporting. For more than 60 years, Fiesta's **Day in Old Mexico** at Rancho del Charro has featured a *charreada,* a traditional Mexican competition said to have inspired the American rodeo. Horse riding, roping, bull riding, pony rides for kids, and *folklorico* performances make for a thrilling day. *Charros* in fitted jackets with detailed embroidery, silk ties, and wide-brimmed sombreros try the *paso de la muerte,* or step of death, galloping on a bare-backed horse and leaping onto another mid-ride. *Colas,* or tails, sees horse riders catch a young bull by the tail, tripping it to allow other riders to administer medicine or tags (if the trick were done on a ranch). Women in elaborate dresses and full skirts ride side saddle at full speed in choreographed formations, showing off their *escaramuza* skills. Expect passionate songs from mariachis at the day-long event as well. Tickets can be purchased for $20 at the gate.

Events at Fiesta range from free to ticketed, with at least half a dozen to choose from

▲ *charros* and *charras* on parade

each day. The online Fiesta calendar is your best resource for finding parade routes and event information. A favorite free event of mine is Fiesta Fiesta at Hemisfair, where you can enjoy live music, dance performances, and fireworks. Check out other free events include Fiesta de la Familia at St. Gregory the Great Catholic Church, the Fiesta of Cascarones at Texas A&M University, and Piñatas in the Barrio in Plaza Guadalupe. Tickets for the big events, like Battle of Flowers, Fiesta Flambeau, and Texas Cavaliers River Parade, can be purchased online ($14-35), with prices tiered by best view of the floats.

Don your traditional Mexican garb, like embroidered dresses called *huipils* or button down *guayaberas,* and plan to eat your way through the street parades. If you've ever been to a Mexican family party, you know that they last long into the night. The nearly two-week event that is Fiesta translates the small party to a city festival worthy of its cultural heritage.

Connect with . . .

㉖ Unwrap an ice-cold *paleta*

㉘ Eat tacos for all three meals

㉜ Shop in "Little Mexico" at San Antonio's Historic Market Square

31 Explore underground at Natural Bridge Caverns

Outdoor Adventures • Hike & Bike • Family Friendly • Day Trips

Why Go: Explore unreasonably gigantic chambers, unexpected natural pools, and strange rock sculptures a few hundred feet below ground.

Where: Natural Bridge Caverns • 26495 Natural Bridge Caverns Rd., San Antonio • 210/651-6101 • https://naturalbridgecaverns.com

Timing: Open every day from 9am until 4pm on weekdays and until 5pm on weekends. Cavern tours depart every 10-40 minutes and typically last an hour. Arrive half an hour before your tour time to check in. Plan for extra time if you want to tackle the surface attractions.

Natural Bridge Caverns are an ancient rock marvel. The caves are mind-blowingly large and intricately formed, where lumpy stalagmites ooze water over pale, yellowish-brown formations. Growing at about one cubic inch every hundred years, these rocks are slow, delicate history.

Natural Bridge Caverns has a mix of cavern tours and surface attractions, including a ropes course, gem and fossil mining, a maze, and climbing wall. A miniature version of the ropes course will enthrall the toddlers. However, the stars of the show here are the underground attractions.

Stroll leisurely on the Discovery Tour, Hidden Passages Tour, or Combo Tour. The caverns sweat, so it's important to wear shoes that won't slip. The popular **Discovery Tour** covers three-quarters of mile in an hour. The **Hidden Passages Tour** is shorter, at a third of a mile, but includes lots of lighting changes and special formations underground. If you don't want to pick, you can do both on the **Combo Tour.** A more active, three-hour private VIP experience, the **Discovery Adventure Tour** provides helmets and headlamps for muddy crawling, climbing, and hiking across half a mile. Crawl spaces are tight at 22 by 14 inches.

Everyone's first adventure is the small corral of check-in lines for purchasing tickets and collecting wristbands before tours. Reservations are recommended for all tours and are required for the Discovery Adventure Tour. Spend $20-28 per person for the more traditional

△ Natural Bridge

cavern tours (there's a discount for booking in advance online). Adventure tours are $399 for two people and $99 for each additional person, up to four total. Once the wrist bands are on, wait outside until your guide rounds everyone up together and begins the tour.

Before embarking on your tour of the underworld, there are a few things to keep in mind. Please don't touch anything but the metal handrails. The oil and bacteria from your skin could prevent the rock from growing. Temperatures will drop quickly and then warm back up for the majority of the tour. At 70% humidity, the cavern feels like a balmy 85 degrees. Also, guides will politely ask you to consider your own level of fitness. Treks are moderately strenuous and sometimes slippery. All tours descend and climb through a series of "rooms" to a depth of about 180 feet, or 18 stories.

Natural Bridge Caverns were explored and turned into a commercial enterprise by students from St. Edward's University. Inside, those students used rock formations they found, and their own college imaginations, to name each section of the cave, or "room." The Bear Pit, the first room you enter after passing the natural limestone bridge at the start of the tour, was

1: descent to the caverns **2:** ropes course **3:** the exit **4:** in the caverns

based on a real 8,000-year-old bear jawbone found inside. Rooms like Pluto's Anterroom, Sherwood Forest, and the Castle of White Giants were also based on the memorable rock formations inside. The formations themselves were also given their own names like The Watchtower, Mount of the Landlord, King's Throne, and The Chandelier.

Families of all ages amble along, single-file, huffing, puffing or skipping joyfully, depending on age and mood, compelled to duck and lean to avoid jutting, sandy-colored rocks at head-level along a few narrow paths. Tour guides raise and dim the lights, revealing the full extent of the underground rooms as you enter and exit. Here, a small pool of water glows bluish-green. There, a room raining small droplets from the roof. Your tour guide will likely point their flashlight to the "cave curtains," sheets of rock undulating back and forth like window dressings. The Chandelier, inside the Castle of White Giants, is an enormous cave curtain, bunched and hanging from the ceiling like a huge octopus. A huge column of rock called The Watchtower stands 50 feet tall and 6 feet wide in the same room. Fairy Castles in the Sherwood Forest room climb 32 feet up, and hollow, thin, soda-straw stalactites are equally impressive, hanging like icicles overhead.

The black spots on the ceiling of one room are an old bat roost. Because the mammals have dirt and bacteria on their skin, nothing will grow from that roost. The final room is the largest, with dimensions of about 250 feet by 100 feet. The formations here took on human-like shapes; a man and a woman huddled together, a woman looking over her shoulder. A line forms at the end of the tour, with each person offering to take photos for the family in front of theirs and snapping pics overlooking the huge cavern below.

Up a ramp lit with Christmas lights and lined with metal handrails, you're left to your own devices to follow a long, covered path back to the surface attractions. Make your way to the small food court to celebrate your conquering of the caverns with a slice of pizza or an ice cream. Or pick up a memento of your journey from one of the gift shops. Who doesn't want a book about bats or a cool geode?

32 Shop in "Little Mexico" at San Antonio's Historic Market Square

Art & Culture • Only in San Antonio • Shopping

Why Go: Enjoy an idyllic slice of Little Mexico, which overflows with ambiance, colorful gifts, and fragrant food hot off the outdoor grills.

Where: Historic Market Square • 514 W Commerce St., San Antonio • 210/207-8600 • www.marketsquaresa.com

Timing: Historic Market Square touts itself as the largest Mexican market in the United States. Spend an hour or two taking it all in, stopping to order a hot plate of tacos or a cold beer cocktail to enjoy while you stroll. Hours of operation vary; check online before you go.

Turn the corner onto Market Square and a flood of color announces a world distinct from everyday San Antonio. *Papel picado,* a Mexican folk craft of tissue paper in vivid colors cut into delicate patterns, is strung across the rooftops and flutters among the trees in this historic plaza. Colorfully painted, adobe-style store fronts line the square, and the brick paths feel like a traditional Mexican home's warm center courtyard.

Historic Market Square was a thriving market in the early 1700s, when "Chili Queens" sold hot bowls of chili from large terracotta pots next to tin lanterns lit with candles. After moving to its current location in the 1890s to make room for settlers during a population boom, the market became a hub for immigrant merchants selling produce until about 1900. It wasn't until the late 1970s that an effort by San Antonio's preservation movement resurrected the space. Today, you'll find over 100 Mexican shops and stalls, but this is no typical flea market.

Accordion-laced Mexican ballads and Tejano hits, the Texan hybrid of Mexican-Spanish and German-Czech music, fill the square. Displays outside the shops offer treasures to be found, like colorful *huipils* (embroidered dresses) I used to love to wear as a kid and backpacks in hot pink, neon yellow, and Tenochtitlan red. I am drawn into the shops by the beautifully embroidered flowers on long tablecloth runners. Rainbows of *calavera* mugs and Talavera lizards

leather purses and toys for sale

micheladas made to order

San Antonio's Historic Market Square

149

▲ colorful walkways decorated with *papel picado*

line the shelves, along with small clay jewelry boxes painted white, turquoise, and magenta. The impulse towards bright colors is an inheritance from local, pre-Columbian traditions.

Folded neatly, *sarapes* (blankets) in earth tones or pastels on sale for only $10 are a steal. Choose your fighter from *lucha libre* masks in kids and adult sizes on display from floor to ceiling. Sombreros sit in stacks on wooden stools, and children's guitars are hung on wire displays. A stack of leather purses engraved with names hang near piles of huarache sandals made out of striped cloth. The huaraches, like many of the other wares, are eye-catching souvenirs from the most colorful regions of Mexico but are not especially practical.

A few stalls sell *micheladas,* beer with lime, tomato juice, and spices in a salt rimmed mug. Tortillas for street tacos are warmed on black *comals,* and balls of masa are smashed down to make *gorditas.* I order one with chicken and refried beans and the cashier tells me that her favorite is *picadillo,* as she loads it up with a guacamole salsa, crema, shredded lettuce, and queso fresco. Some stands offer churros, serving the fried treat rolled in cinnamon and sugar, while others sell *aguas frescas,* a fruity drink available in flavors like pineapple, watermelon, cantaloupe, and cucumber.

I am aware of the high tourist-value of the plaza, but I am drawn deeper, sending photos to my friends to ask if they find the space as impressive as I do, or if I'm just not used to Mexican markets. They reply immediately that the scenes reflect the beauty of their beloved mother-country and ask me for more details on the place.

San Antonians keep strong familial, religious, and lingual ties to Mexico, and Market Square collects the country's prettiest charms in rainbow colors, suggesting love and appreciation. Like the symbolic snakes painted on jewelry boxes, the square has shed old skin. From a working immigrant's fresh food market to a flowery showpiece for gifts and trinkets, this little Mexico has transformed. Spanish is still spoken. Tex-Mex is still served. But the produce has moved out and the souvenirs have moved in. Bring a bag for your armfuls of new knick-knacks and gifts for friends. The urge to redecorate in humming, expressionist shades comes on strong.

Connect with . . .
26 Unwrap an ice-cold *paleta*
30 Wear a flower crown at Fiesta

33 See the best of old and new San Antonio in the Pearl District

Why Go: Wander through restaurants, shops, and a weekly farmers market in a European-feeling plaza in this historic district.

Where: Pearl District is a clump of winding streets and pedestrian walkways north of downtown San Antonio, bordered by the San Antonio River to the west and Freeway 281 to the east. Visit https://atpearl.com to learn more.

Timing: Plan half a day at this historic center to enjoy a meal and explore the area. Visit midmorning on Saturdays and Sundays for the farmers market.

The historic, architectural soul of San Antonio, the revitalized and spit-shined Pearl District comes with stories of famous brewers and their business savvy through Prohibition. More than

▲ Pearl Beer used to be bottled here.

a wild historical story, San Antonio's Pearl District is an invitation to a convivial atmosphere, where people leisurely sit on patios and enjoy the weather, sip coffee or cocktails, and shop at the farmers market on weekends. This space encourages visitors to just be, without the usual pressures to shop or move along. Whether you'd like to stay in the historic hotel for a weekend or visit for a day, you can count on the best of old and new San Antonio at the Pearl District.

Start at the front entrance to the **Hotel Emma** (136 E Grayson St., 844/845-7384, www.thehotelemma.com) at the end of Isleta Street near the roundabout made of a stainless-steel hopper covered in lush, overflowing greenery. The tallest building in San Antonio when it was completed in 1894, Hotel Emma used to be the brew house for one of the largest breweries in Texas, Pearl Brewery. Pearl beer was brewed and bottled in this complex until 2001. Now the restored Hotel Emma is the crown jewel of the neighborhood.

Intrigue surrounds the Hotel Emma, named for Emma Koehler. Emma ran the brewery after her husband Otto Koehler, the former President of Pearl, died in 1914. Otto was murdered

▲ pecans for sale at the farmers market

▲ sunset at Hotel Emma

▲ The Pearl

at the hands of one of his two mistresses, who were each also named Emma. Emma Koehler then shrewdly pivoted Pearl's operations, keeping the enterprise afloat through Prohibition. Once Prohibition ended, the Pearl brewery was immediately up and running. An old photo shows trucks being loaded with deliveries of the beer one minute after midnight on the day Prohibition was over.

Do not skip a walk through Hotel Emma, because the building has been thoughtfully restored outside and in. Iron trusses, high ceilings, and exposed brick are paired with leather seats, concrete columns, and brass details. A massive old ammonia compressor (formerly used to cool beer) still sits on the lobby floor, and antique brewery pipes run half the height of the walls in some areas. Down the halls and corridors are placards and old photos explaining how the building's use evolved over time. Today, there are more than a couple of excellent restaurants inside Hotel Emma, including my favorite, **Southerleigh Fine Food and Brewery** (210/455-5701, www.southerleighatpearl.com).

Exit through the back of the hotel and you'll find yourself in a European-feeling plaza. Surrounded by smaller structures, the entire complex reflects the work of Rundbogenstil architects, who used the German Romanesque revival style to demonstrate the pride of the German brewers in the area. The hotel lends a grand old-world flare to the plaza behind it, where people lounge in a turf park. Walk around the park to the building that says **"Food Hall"** in big capital letters. This was the site of the original bottling building for Pearl Brewery until a fire in 2004. The long, rectangular building was rebuilt with the original bottling plant as inspiration. Inside, you'll find a full bar with Texas beers, including Pearl beer, and a handful of eateries, like Asian noodle purveyor **Tenko Ramen** (210/ 267-2996, www.tenkoramen.com), Mexican street food at **Chilaquil** (210/267-1125, https://eatchilaquil.com), and thrilling Caribbean flavors at **Mi Roti** (www.miroti210.com). Pay inside, then step outside to the patio tables or spread out over the green lawn in the plaza.

On Saturdays and Sundays, there's an outdoor **farmers market** focusing on local Texas vendors who set up around the green turf space of the plaza. The offerings are oriented towards unique prepared foods and less on fresh produce. Swift River Pecans from Fentress sells buttery pecan oil and varieties of the nut, and Bending Branch Winery from Comfort sells bottles of a unique Tannat grape varietal alongside the popular Texas Tempranillo. Lines form for freshly prepared empanadas, and you'll find rice pudding and dry Spanish chorizo at booths at this market as well.

Once you've had your fill, head west of the Emma to the **River Walk,** where the San Antonio River moves past a terraced amphitheater. Live Latin alternative bands grace the stage here, and free movies are screened periodically. Check the Pearl website for more information. In the absence of special programming, grab a seat to watch local neighborhood street performers practice on the stage. From here, you can stroll south along the River Walk until your hearts content (the walk goes on for 15 miles).

A German Brewmeister named the Pearl district for the bubbles in the beer (they looked like pearls to him). More than 100 years later, the name has seen scandal, success, and wild swings of fate, surviving the teetotalling years of the roaring 20s. The European style square today is a perfect place for a family outing, top-tier meal, or cocktail date.

Connect with . . .

36 Take in art along River Walk

37 Walk in tranquility at the Japanese Tea Garden

34 Bike the Mission Trail

Outdoor Adventures • Hike & Bike • Only in San Antonio • Art & Culture

Why Go: Pedal back in time approximately 300 years as you explore the only UNESCO World Heritage Site in Texas.

Where: San Antonio Missions National Historic Park • https://www.nps.gov

Timing: Plan at least four hours to bike the trail and stop at each mission. If you go during summer, start early in the morning to avoid the worst of the heat.

I am racing against the sun with my friend Ursula. August is traditionally one of the hottest months in San Antonio. The temperature should reach 102 degrees Fahrenheit by noon. We plan to bike to four Spanish colonial missions along the paved hike-and-bike Mission Trail that hugs the San Antonio River. At 8:30am, we arrive at **Blue Star Arts Complex** (125 Blue Star 6). It's located near the start of the trail, north of Mission Concepción. There's a convenient bike rental shop and a bank of B-Cycle bike rentals. Ursula and I have hats, snacks, water, and sunscreen—all the essentials. Each mission is about 2.5 miles from the next, and the final stretch is mostly uphill. The air is cooler by the water, but there are also long sunny stretches that bake our backs. Ursula's been to the missions before, so she navigates with the help of signposts as guides.

▲ biking the Mission Trails

First up: imposing **Mission Concepción** (807 Mission Rd.), or Nuestra Señora de la Purísima Concepción, with two belfry towers and a dome over the center of the cruciform layout. It's considered the best-preserved mission in Texas, nearly unrestored aside from the dome, which was reinforced in early 2020. Construction began in East Texas but was moved to San Antonio in 1731. The mission, built of limestone rubble and plaster covered with sculpted stone, was completed in 1755. The once brightly painted façade has faded over the centuries. Every 15th of August, a double illumination occurs: The sun shines into the church, illuminat-

Mission Concepción

Mission Espada

Mission San Juan Capistrano

ing the center of the floor shaped like a cross, and the face of the Virgin Mary behind the altar. It's one of the largest missions, along with Mission San José, which we ride to next.

Finished in 1782, **Mission San José y San Miguel de Aguayo** (6701 San Jose Dr.) is jaw-dropping, with intricately carved colonnades, cherubs, and saints on the façade. If you can only visit one mission, this is the one to see. Restored in the 1930s, the Baroque church is

▲ Mission San José y San Miguel de Aguayo

picturesque and especially dramatic when the clear ringing of its bells fills the air. Pale blue geometric designs on white plaster on the church's outer walls hint at how the frescos once gleamed in the sun. On one side of the church there are huge arches and abundant green plants. The church was the center of a village which included a farm, a ranch, and artisan workshops for carpenters, weavers, and a blacksmith. Stopping for photos, we duck under the shade of barrel vault archways, chatting with other cyclists. Just like us, one rider is a local showing an out-of-towner the sights, and we ride next to each other the rest of the way.

Our next stop, **Mission San Juan Capistrano** (9101 Graf Rd.), is unfinished. Building halted in 1787 because there was not enough labor or money to continue, but extensive repairs in 2011 created the gleaming white walls we see today. Minimal compared to the other missions, the restored church is still visually striking, although it is not the first or only church built on the grounds. The original structure was made of straw and mud. It was replaced with a second adobe church, long and low like the current one. This third, larger church remains incomplete. This mission complex is surrounded by acres of space, lending a gravity to the area instead of crowding the ruins.

The southernmost stop on the trail is **Mission Espada** (10040 Espada Rd.). The name refers to the *espadanas,* or bell gables, on top of the church. It was completed in 1777; only the original façade dates back to that time. The grounds are expertly manicured, with red bird of paradise in bloom. Soldiers once used sculptured saints as target practice and tourists of the past took relics or pieces of mission church doors. Today, most traveling pilgrims stop into the gift shop and pay for souvenirs, or leave only coins to light votives inside the prayer rooms. The Catholic Archdiocese has led the preservation movement to maintain and respect the missions as religious, historic spaces.

Ursula and I sit on a bench outside eating trail mix and chocolate from our backpacks, tired from the ride. It's easy to get caught up in the imposing architecture and intricate artwork, but we think for a moment what this display of Spanish power must have looked like to the Indigenous people. The missions were built with the purpose of converting the local population to Christianity. Historians tell us that many of those people were enslaved to work the land and build these mission complexes. Many of these Indigenous people did not survive; entire communities and cultures were wiped out. To learn more about the dark and complicated history of the missions, visit www.sanantonio.gov.

Connect with . . .

26 Unwrap an ice-cold *paleta*

28 Eat tacos for all three meals

35 Stroll through King William Historic District

Neighborhoods & City Streets • Art & Culture

Why Go: Mansions built here in the late 1800s are a sight to behold. Add a few open gardens, house tours, and art galleries for a perfect morning stroll.

Where: Five blocks of historic homes stretch from East Guenther Street near the San Antonio River to South St. Mary's Street.

Timing: Plan on two hours. Most gardens and museums close by 3pm, so get an early start at the Blue Star Arts Complex, then take in King William Street. End with lunch on Alamo Street. Not all mansions and gardens are open every day, but most can be visited on Saturdays. Verify hours in advance.

Welcome to the 1800s! First settled by well-to-do German immigrants, this neighborhood was originally nicknamed "Sauerkraut Bend." The mid-1800s saw dozens of three-story homes built in Victorian, French Renaissance, and Greek Revival styles, so it became better known by the statelier name "King William District." In 1968, the neighborhood was designated as the city's first historic district. By then, it had gone from fashionable to not so fashionable and back again; this time residents were intent on preserving the elegant, eclectic architecture they considered their heritage. (And yes, many of the houses are said to be haunted.)

Begin just a stone's throw away at the hip **Blue Star Arts Complex** (125 Blue Star 6, San Antonio, 210/354-3775, https://bluestarartscomplex.com) on the River Walk. This revitalized warehouse with contemporary art galleries, restaurants, and coffee shops is a Swiss Army knife of cool. Sip coffee on the patio at **Halcyon** (414 S Alamo St., 210/277-7045, http://halcyoncoffeebar.com), then stop by **Blue Star Contemporary,** (116 Blue Star, 210/227-6960, https://bluestarcontemporary.org), the first of many modern art spaces in San Antonio.

From Halcyon on the corner of South Alamo Street, turn right to cross the bridge over the river. Turn left on Guenther Street and then right on King William Street. Immediately on your left, you'll see the **Edward Steves Homestead Museum** (509 King William St., 210/227-9160, www.saconservation.org), three stories of pure style built in 1876 by English architect

Villa Finale Museum & Gardens

George Chabot House

Alfred Giles for a German lumber don. Behold the mansard roof with delicate French iron cresting atop the house. Self-guided walking tours are available on weekends for $10. Just across the street on the next block, **Edward Steves Jr. House** (431 King William St.) features lovely bay windows and patterned decorative scrollwork. Next up, the **George Kalteyer House** (425 King William St.) has almost a dozen stone arches in alternating colors. The house was divided into apartments until the historic district was established and restoration began. At one time, a fire escape arched from the left turret down to the front lawn. Next door, walk the manicured gardens of the **Villa Finale Museum & Garden** (401 King William St., 210/223-9800, www. villafinale.org, free). If you have time, head into the house ($5) to view the gorgeous art.

A quick detour onto Turner Street takes you past King Williams Park to **Oge House** (209 Washington St.). This neoclassical, white two-story mansion allegedly has a kitchen ghost that blows away seasonings she prefers not to be used. Book a stay via AirBnB to gather evidence of this spectral presence. Walk back down Turner Street and turn left on Madison Street to stop at the free **San Antonio Art League & Museum** (130 King William St., 210/223-1140,

▲ the San Antonio River

Celebrate

The Blue Star Arts Complex is a great jumping-off point for the monthly free **First Friday Art Walk** (https://southtownsatx.com), which showcases Southtown's art scene. Expect open exhibits, vendors, and live music along S Alamo Street and St. Mary's Street.

The annual **Sauerkraut Bend 5k** benefits the local neighborhood. A costume contest crowns the best dressed King and Queen, who run in their regal attire. Sausage, sauerkraut, and beer are served.

https://www.saalm.org), for contemporary work by Texas artists like Keith McIntyre and Amy Freeman Lee.

Walk southwest down Madison Street to see another stretch of beautiful homes. Keep an eye out for the elegant **George Chabot house** (403 Madison St.), with delicate verandas, and the **Berman/Kinder House** (338 Madison St.) with a curving front porch and large staircases leading to the front door.

When Madison Street ends, make a left on Gunther Street and another left on S Alamo Street to find an abundance of restaurants. In good weather, eat on the patio table at **The Friendly Spot** (943 S Alamo St., 210/224-2337, thefriendlyspot.com) or splurge at **Little Em's Oyster Bar** (1001 S Alamo St., 210/257-0100, www.littleemsoysterbar.com).

Connect with . . .

26 Unwrap an ice-cold *paleta*

27 Immerse yourself in art at Hopscotch

34 Bike the Mission Trail

36 Take in art along the River Walk

Art & Culture • Only in San Antonio • Neighborhoods & City Streets

Why Go: The River Walk alternates tropical green space, meditative stretches, and lively restaurants, but the real gem is the art you find along the way. It starts weird and ends wild.

Where: Start at The Grotto, near Camden Street Bridge, in the Museum Reach section of the River Walk, and stroll two miles south to end at the San Fernando Cathedral in the Historic Downtown portion.

Timing: Start out a few hours before dinner to ramble and dine on the river, then catch the light show at the San Fernando Cathedral at 9pm, 9:30pm, or 10pm on Tuesday, Friday, Saturday, and Sunday.

Adorned with mosaics, installations of giant glowing fish, and surreal grottos, San Antonio's River Walk is full of surprises, making this winding pedestrian river path feel enchanted. The

The Grotto by Carlos Cortés

River Walk spans 15-miles of the city, five of which course through the heart of downtown, below street-level. The walk is a must-see in the city and a great way to navigate the sights. To take in the art, start in the Museum Reach section of the walk and wind a few miles south to downtown. Endless dining options crowd this popular area of the river, where you can eat an early dinner before watching a mesmerizing light show projected onto the oldest cathedral in Texas.

Start north of downtown by Camden and Newell Streets. Walk down the stairs and into the mouth of a yawning jaguar to enter the underground world of **The Grotto.** Third generation faux-bois artist Carlos Cortés used concrete to create a convincing organic cave. Summer greenery makes this tunneled chasm look bright, but the cave feels alive all year. Walking through the tunneled passageway, keep an eye out for stalactites, waterfalls, and Father Nature's giant head spewing water. The tunnel deposits you onto the River Walk. As you exit and continue making your way

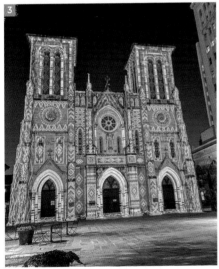

1: mosaics by Oscar Alvarado **2:** *F.I.S.H.* by Donald Lipski **3:** *The Saga* by Xavier de Richemont, projected on the San Fernando Cathedral **4:** San Antonio's River Walk along the river, look to your right and see Mother Nature represented in the negative space inside a tall rock formation.

Seven-foot-long orange and blue fish are just five minutes south. Suspended in the air just under the Interstate Highway 35 overpass, the giant models of longear sunfish will make you feel like a tiny undersea creature beneath them. Real longear sunfish are only a few inches long and are native to the San Antonio River. Donald Lipski's *F.I.S.H.* glow at night but are still spectacular when they glimmer in the sunshine.

Continue south from here, and cross over the skinny, delicate-looking **Ewing Halsell Pedestrian Bridge** to the east side of the river and keep heading south past the paddling ducks and sunbathing turtles. The history of the Yanaguana, the original name for the San Antonio River area given by the Indigenous Payaya people, is explained on mounted plaques as you move south.

Walk almost a mile down to McCullough Street, where a series of **mosaics** were created by San Antonio's self-taught artist Oscar Alvarado. A portrait of José Antonio Navarro memorializes the leader who fought for Texan independence and who was one of the first signers of the Texas Declaration of Independence. A map of the city, a map of the river, and several other mosaics along the walk were also created by Navarro. His work creates moments of unexpected charm under bridges between Richmond and Travis Streets, often using a cool color palette that complements the emerald waters running nearby.

The River Walk becomes more tropical as it approaches downtown. Banana, papaya, and lemon trees frame twisting stone stairways and arching bridges. You'll know you've hit downtown when you get see busy restaurant patios. Shops sell beers and margaritas for tourists to carry around as they stroll (drinking in public is ok if you stay below street-level). I recommend **Acenar** (146 E Houston St., 210/222-2362, https://acenar.com) for delicious Tex-Mex with a great view. Or visit **The Esquire Tavern** (155 E Commerce St., 210/222-2521, www.esquire-tavern-sa.com), the oldest bar on the River Walk, for great cocktails with dinner.

While you can head directly to the Main Plaza after dinner, I recommend taking a quick, 15-minute detour to walk through the heart of the River Walk. Where the river splits, just north of Commerce Street Bridge, take the left fork and make your way east, following the original path of the river as it makes a u-shape. Pass colorful restaurants and electric boats shuttling tourists as you make a loop back towards Commerce Street. Come up to street level just past the bridge.

The Main Plaza, between Commerce and Dolorosa Streets, is home to the oldest cathedral in Texas, **San Fernando Cathedral** (115 N Main Ave., 210/225-9800, www.mainplaza.org) where French artist Xavier de Richemont created a free, stellar light show shown on the towering 7,000 square foot façade. Playing three times a night on the weekends and Tuesdays, ***The Saga*** recounts the history of Texas from pre-Columbian times to the present. A loud thunderclap starts the light show and continues with scenes of sea monsters, buffalo, beadwork, saints, battles, chains, flags, *mercados*, flowers, and more. A dynamic and varied soundtrack accompanies the roughly half hour long chromatic projection.

Like a secret journey through a labyrinth, the River Walk is quiet on the north end and bustling with people downtown. The fee for the hallowed ground is taken at the pricey restaurants and bars, though the ambiance is free. Public art installations transform plain underpasses and sidewalks, making the River Walk feel like a tropical oasis in a concrete city.

Connect with . . .

- **27** Immerse yourself in art at Hopscotch
- **29** Get spooked on a ghost tour
- **30** Wear a flower crown at Fiesta
- **33** See the best of old and new San Antonio in the Pearl District
- **35** Stroll through King William Historic District

37 Walk in tranquility at the Japanese Tea Garden

Art & Culture

Why Go: Walk the stone bridges and winding pathways of the free historic Japanese Tea Garden to find koi ponds, sunken gardens, and a cascading waterfall.

Where: Japanese Tea Garden • Brackenridge Park, 3853 N Saint Mary's St., San Antonio • 210/559-3148 • https://japaneseteagardensa.org

Timing: The Japanese Tea Garden is open daily from dawn to dusk, but you'll only need an hour to enjoy roaming the manicured grounds. The garden is well-trafficked on the weekends, making weekdays a quieter time to visit.

Patterned in bright strokes of red on snowy white flesh, koi glide past in the shallow pond. Known as "living flowers," the fish are an essential part of the Japanese Tea Garden. Nestled in Brackenridge Park, their garden home offers a tranquil place to escape to in the middle of the city.

Past the entrance gate, a large pagoda overlooks the entire garden. Manicured green shrubs in rounded shapes form gentle hills alongside the delicate blooms of blue plumbago, lilies, and other lush foliage packed tightly together. Snap a few photos here before walking down the stone steps to visit the garden and the lily ponds below. Here you can wander across low bridges gracefully arching over small, koi-filled ponds. Check out the serene Platinum Ogon, immaculate white koi, as they swim nearby the brown-bronze Chagoi, friendly koi decorated with delicate scale patterns. You'll also spot the eye-catching Yamabuki Ogon koi, with its solid metallic yellow hue. Winding paths and short stairways lead to the 60-foot waterfall set against a beautiful mossy background. Shaded footpaths offer a glimpse at what the Japanese call *komorebi,* or light peeking through the leaves.

This park has a long history, one that reflects the story of Asian minorities in the United States who have been alternately sought for labor and then rejected in xenophobic waves of anger. Rolling bridges edged in roughhewn stone recall the park's past as a rock quarry that helped produce limestone for some of San Antonio's earliest buildings, including the Menger

▲ the view looking out from the large central pavilion

▲ waterfall

▲ Japanese Tea Garden

Hotel. The land was donated to the city in 1899. In an attempt to keep costs as low as possible, City Parks Commissioner Ray Lambert used prison labor to convert the land into a garden, building walkways and bridges. The project was completed in 1917.

Lambert worked with World War I veteran and watercolor artist Eizo "Kimi" Jingu to design the garden. Born in Japan, Kimi immigrated to the United States in the early 1900s, where he met his wife Miyoshi and moved to San Antonio after his time in the army. Lambert later invited Kimi Jingu to move in with his family and to become caretakers for the garden. In 1926, Jingu's family moved into a small house on the grounds, where they oversaw the park and served lunch to visitors. Kimi's children later recounted their unique memories from life in the Japanese Tea Garden, especially with regards to the zoo next door. Their mother would tell them that the zoo lions would roar their loudest whenever it was going to rain. There are also stories of a monkey who escaped from the zoo and visited the garden, where he was given a piece of gum. The monkey was recaptured but made chewing gestures at the Jingu kids whenever they would later pass his cage in the zoo. After Kimi died, his widow and children were

koi pond

evicted in 1941 and the park was renamed the Chinese Tea Garden due to the anti-Japanese sentiment of World War II. The original name was restored in 1984, and Jingu family descendants attended the renaming ceremony.

Next to the grand, stacked stone pagoda, The Jingu House, formerly the family's home, is now a tiny casual café serving light lunches of bento boxes, sushi, salads, and wraps. Pastry lovers can snag a lemon bar or other dessert from the display case above the bottled drinks. A few tables outside the café are the only seating, so grab an iced tea and take it with you to enjoy as you walk the Garden grounds.

The only animal life in the park on most days are the Japanese koi. Almost glowing, these fish can live up to fifty years, and symbolize tenacity and fortitude. But the rare rainy-day visitor can still listen for the lions next door.

Connect with . . .

33 See the best of old and new San Antonio in the Pearl District
36 Take in art along the River Walk

38 Float the river in San Marcos

Why Go: Nothing soothes a hot summer day like floating the crystal-clear San Marcos River.

Where: Thirty miles southwest of Austin, the city of San Marcos offers multiple access points along the San Marcos River, as well as different outfitters where you can rent your float gear.

Timing: Floating is a summer activity, when outfitters are open daily and people flock to the river, especially on weekends. Some outfitters are open year-round but with limited availability. River floats typically take one to three hours, with the last shuttle back to your car leaving between 4:30pm and 7:30pm. Check your specific rental location for timing.

It's time to earn your float badge in San Marcos. The city is 30 miles south of Austin and is synonymous with lazing along the river in an inflated tube. Locals will bring their favorite "river

floating the river

beer," which is shorthand for cheap, light lagers that go down like water in the summer sun. Fancy beer from craft breweries is allowed, too. Your main job on the river is to keep ahold of that one beer or your favorite canned sparkling water (I'm partial to anything black cherry flavored), and dangle the other hand languidly over the other edge of your tube, flapping at the water intermittently to steer.

People will say that a good burn is the best "base tan," but I'd question that. Sunscreen is essential, but anything you can put between the sun and your face, like sunglasses or hats, is a great idea. Wear your swimsuit, and don't bring anything you can't comfortably watch float away. Rubber-soled water shoes protect your feet from anything sharp in the water, plus there's no risk losing them in the river. Throw water and your preferred river beer in a cooler, toss it into a tube with a bottom (or use an inflatable cooler), and lash it to your tube so you stay fully

the San Marcos River

mountain of inner tubes

a clear day on the river

stocked for the entire float. Glass is a big no-no anywhere near the water, but so is, surprisingly, drinking any alcoholic beverage when not strictly in the river. Thus, pop your top only once you've set sail. Throw your phone in a dry bag and you're all set.

The San Marcos River is free for public use, so if you have your own tube, you can slip into the river at more than a dozen access points, which are mapped by the city's Parks and Recreation department (www.sanmarcostx.gov). The one catch is that you'll need to find a way back to your own car. Otherwise, take your tube to one of the outfitters mentioned below, where you can pay to use their shuttle service.

Each tube rental location provides a tube and a shuttle ride back once you're done. **Lions Club Tube Rental** (San Marcos City Park, 512/396-5466, www.tubesanmarcos.com) caters to families with children with a one-hour float for $14 per person that includes a tube and unlimited shuttle rides. If you want to drop in with your own tube, pay $10 for access to the shuttle. **Great Gonzo's Tubes** (19385 San Marcos Hwy., 512/749-2991, https://greatgonzostubes. com) charges $8 for shuttle rides and $10 per tube rental on its one and a half to two-hour float,

▲ Floating in a double tube is double the fun!

Celebrate

Each June, the San Marcos River is home to the **Texas Water Safari** (www.texaswa-tersafari.org). Also known as the world's toughest canoe race, the 260-mile course from San Marcos to the Texas coastline has been testing people since 1963.

plus you get a free bottomed-tube when you rent four regular tubes. If you'd like a ride from Austin to San Marcos, you can make an advance reservation with **Texas State Tubes** (2024 N Old Bastrop Hwy., 512/638-7165, https://texasstatetubes.com). For $55, you can be picked up at 11am from downtown Austin and driven back around 4pm, after a three-hour trip on the river. Alternatively, you can rent a tube in San Marcos for $25, including a shuttle ride. Drop-ins with their own tubes pay $15 for a shuttle back. It's a great idea to reserve your tube online before you head out, or at least call to make sure there are enough tubes available for walk-up renters that day.

The main thing to remember is that this is a summer activity. College kids are really into it, and Texas State University has about 40,000 students, so you'll be in lots of young company. But families are also welcome. Groups tend stay together, pausing where the water is shallow to regroup. The shores are privately owned, so you have to stay in the water while you float. The San Marcos River is 72 degrees year-round and crystal clear, making it Texas' perfect lazy river.

Connect with . . .

41 Paint the town red at the oldest dancehall in Texas
47 Drink with the devil at the Devil's Backbone Tavern

39 Fire an apple cannon at a fall festival

Outdoor Adventures • Family Friendly • Day Trips • Best in Fall

Why Go: Farms around Austin take on a pumpkin spice flare every fall. Corn mazes, pumpkin patches, petting zoos, and so much more make for the perfect family adventure.

Where: Drive 30 mins to an hour out of Austin to get to the farms.

Timing: Plan to spend two to three hours at the farms to take advantage of all the activities, longer if you plan to eat there. Festivities start mid-September at Sweet Berry Farm and Sweet Eats Fruit Farm, and Barton Hills Farm joins in early October. All three stay open until early November, but pumpkins will have all but disappeared by Halloween.

Little silver pails of red apples empty one by one as the fruit is loaded, aimed, and shot from giant sling shots at scarecrow targets in the distance. The result is a beautiful contrast of green grass scattered with red fruit that reminded me of a scene from *The Wizard of Oz*. Remember when the trees throw apples at Dorothy and the Scarecrow? That's the one.

Farms around Austin transform into outdoor playlands in the fall, hosting fall festivals with huge pumpkin patches, giant corn mazes, hayrides, peddle go-karts, petting zoos, and the aforementioned apple cannons. The list of attractions goes on. All ages are welcomed, and all ages attend in costume, especially on Halloween weekend. To see pumpkin patches in their full glory, plan a visit a few weeks before Halloween.

The self-proclaimed "most picturesque farm," **Barton Hills Farm** (1115 FM-969, Bastrop, 855/969-1115, https://bartonhillfarms.com) is like a music festival training camp. Set across a sprawling piece of land, this farm has all the signs of a music fest. If you've been to Austin City Limits at 3pm on a Friday, you've got the right idea. Weekend live music stages? Check. Beer and sangria on sale? Check. Picnic tables in the shade and light concessions? Check.

At Barton, apples are launched from "cannons." Plop an apple down into a small shoot, pull back a metal lever, and fire! The apples hit a metal disk in the distance and explode on con-

getting lost in the corn maze at Barton Hill Farms

apple slingshot at Sweet Eats Fruit Farm

corn maze at Sweet Berry Farm in Marble Falls

▲ pumpkin patch at Barton Hills Farm

tact. Aiming is allegedly possible with this pinball machine on steroids. Apple ammo is a couple extra dollars separate from the cost of admission.

When I visited, I heard a little boy shout "I wanna get lost!" as his family walked into the maze. A cornfield lifeguard sits perched above the center of the maze to help anyone who gets stuck, but the maze was on the kiddie end of challenging as far as mazes go. It was allegedly shaped like Scooby Doo, though who could really tell from inside the "walls" of dry stalks and silk spider webs? The Barton Hills maze is not super high or dense, but in 2pm broad daylight, when I stepped on the dry end of a fallen stalk and the other end rustled two yards away, my friend and I both jumped.

The pièce de résistance at **Sweet Eats Fruit Farm** (14400 E State Highway 29, Georgetown, 512/766-3276, www.sweeteats.com) is the pitch-dark corn maze. Sweet Eats stays open past sundown until 10pm to let families navigate their way in the dark using only a flashlight at night for extra spooky fun around Halloween. Two mazes side by side are created with kids and adults in mind, respectively. Festival goers of all ages flock to this farm in costume for Halloween, from baby cowardly lions to the caped superheroes who carry them. For less labyrinthine fun, Sweet Eats giant tire mountain climbs to a slide at the summit, which is the most efficient way back down. The most adorable little round pigs roam nearby, munching their snacks off the ground. That Wizard of Oz field of sling-shot apples also lives at this farm, next to a stage for live music, and around the corner from a push-peddle go-kart track you can run until your legs give out.

Sweet Berry Farm (1801 FM 1980 Marble Falls, 830/798-1462, https://sweetberryfarm. com) also designed separate mazes for kiddos and adults. The smaller kid's mazes take 15-20 minutes and the adults around an hour to navigate. The friendly corn maze guard warned that no one stays behind waiting for the adult maze to clear, so start early or get lost at your own risk. Hungry goats eat from your hand here, and pumpkin painting produces expressionist pieces in fresh, wet paint to dry and display for decorative gourd season. Kids can also ride ponies here, jump on a berry bounce, and stuff scarecrows, too.

From the apple cannons to the corn maze, this child-at-heart adult recommends trying all the activities, as well as the archery, where you can shoot bales of hay with safely blunted arrows and possibly dull aim. Don't forget to toss the bean bags, swing the lassos, and stop for a beer. Each farm sells pumpkins, of course, and some allow you to pick fresh flowers. If you end up with a handful of Texas blooms, sniff them for a moment, and consider yourself lucky. They get picked fast.

40 Drink ancient desert spirits

Sip Something Strong

Why Go: The first sotol distiller in Texas—and the only one in the country—is reviving a 300-year-old antique desert alcohol. This subtle, faceted spirit sings in delicious cocktails served in a chic Driftwood tasting room where you can be a part of its renaissance.

Where: Desert Door Distillery • 211 Darden Hill Rd., Driftwood • 512/829-6129 • www.desertdoor.com

Timing: Lunchtime is the perfect arrival time, as Desert Door closes by 8pm Thursday-Saturday and at 6 pm on Sunday. Tours are offered Friday-Sunday at noon and 1pm for $10.

Relish a bold, unique Texas cocktail in a comfortable, contemporary tasting room. Old *sotoleros* say the drink should be sipped from a hollow bull's horn, but today the spirit is served in polished cocktail glasses at high end bars around the world. From the lowest rung of the Mexican distiller's ladder, sotol is making a comeback. Austin Mayor Steve Adler even proclaimed November 16 Texas Sotol Day. Mexico says it should only come from their country—like tequila—but three Texas entrepreneurs are claiming the right to take part in the sotol revival. Their distillery, Desert Door, is the first commercial sotol distillery in Texas and the only one making sotol in the United States.

For decades, sotol was outlawed, bootlegged, and smuggled, despite being used by Indigenous people for medicinal and nutritional purposes for thousands of years. The Mexican government violently discouraged distilling by jailing or kidnapping *sotoleros*. There have been many attempts to erase sotol, whether to end competition with the "higher-end" spirits whose profits went to the moneyed classes or to practice strict Prohibition, but small *sotoleros* kept the tradition alive. In the 1990s, Mexico allowed legal production. Slowly, the regional drink has become a new source of pride.

Desert Door started as a University of Texas MBA class project. Judson Kauffman, Ryan

sotol hearts

Desert Door bottle ready to be poured

Desert Door tasting room

Campbell, and Brent Looby started with a pressure cooker, a woodchipper, a 15-gallon still from eBay, and a dream. Today, they have a contemporary tasting room, accented in Southwestern leather and cowhide, complete with a fireplace and a large, covered patio.

Desert Door's **distillery tour** starts with the sotol plant, *Dasylirion texanum*. A long, tall stalk grows straight up like a cream-colored monster asparagus, and the plant spreads wild and "pestilent" at a near-thousand per acre, according to general manager David Vincent. Desert Door harvests their plants wild, only in west Texas deserts, and only when the plant is 10-12 years old. The root system in left intact so that the plant can regenerate, and the "heart" is carted back to the distillery in Driftwood. Stainless-steel baskets hold the 15,000-25,000 pounds of raw hearts that arrive each week. After steaming, smashing, fermenting, and distilling the hearts in large vats with big metal machines, the sotol is bottled in blue porcelain and sold.

Walking through the distillery, the air smells of raisins. "We thought it smelled like graham cracker in here last week," says Vincent. Sotol lovers say it tastes like the desert after the rain hits. The tour comes with a **tasting** of the original and oak-aged sotols in small glasses

▲ the bar at Desert Door

that look like the tops of oil-burning lamps. Fans talk about distinct terroir flavor in this spirit. It's piney near the woods or minerally in the desert. To experiment, Desert Door collaborated on a controlled burn in west Texas, harvesting the sotol plants to make a bottle dubbed "Back Burn." Silver sotol is the main offering, though the sweet and dark barrel-aged version is worth trying as well.

If **cocktails** are more your speed, you're set. Desert Door sotols are not smokey, so they mix like vodka, gin, rum, whiskey, or tequila. Vincent recommended the Comanchero, a cocktail of silver sotol with raw, unfermented sotol nectar on ice with lime and agave. The nectar has a salty, umami flavor, balanced by sweetness from the agave. Other favorites include Ranch Water (sotol with Texas' favorite Mexican sparkling water Topo Chico and lime), Palomas (sotol instead of the traditional tequila and grapefruit juice), and Sotol'd Fashioned, which mimics the classic whiskey drink.

Outside, the food truck **Eden West** (http://edenwestfoodtruck.com) serves food, like butternut queso with chile powder-dusted tortilla chips. The truck is an offshoot of the now shuttered but memorably fantastic farm-to-table restaurant in Austin, Eden East. Sotol nectar is used in its prime rib with onion rings and other offerings. Eden West serves brunch from noon to 2pm on the weekends.

The subtle, versatile spirit resisted outlaw status and suppression to arrive stylishly poured in a minimal, Southwestern-chic Driftwood tasting room today. Whether the antique spirit becomes as ubiquitous as tequila is anyone's guess, so don't miss your chance to be a part of sotol's elegant rebirth.

Connect with . . .

50 Sip liquid sunshine on the Texas Whiskey Trail

41

Paint the town red at the oldest dancehall in Texas

Nightlife • Getaway

Why Go: Escape to Gruene for dinner and a show at Texas' oldest continuously operating dancehall, then spend the night in an old bed and breakfast before strolling the historic town in the morning.

Where: Gruene Historic District in New Braunfels, about 45 minutes south of Austin

Timing: Gruene is close enough to visit for the evening, but the dinner, drinks, and country music dancehall beg you stay the night in a fancy old B&B after going out.

Gruene, Texas (pronounced "green") does not technically exist, but don't let that deter you from visiting. Forgotten and nearly bulldozed to make way for condos in the 1970s, Gruene survived a few twists of fate to become a picturesque historic district in New Braunfels. A handsome slice of Texas past, Gruene is the legacy of a mid-1800s German settlement. Across 20-odd acres within a stone's throw of the flowing Guadalupe River, Gruene has a lot to offer, including live music at Texas' oldest dancehall, restaurants and wine tasting rooms, and historic buildings packed with antiques and souvenirs.

German immigrants descended on the town formerly known as Goodwin to farm their own piece of the American dream. Enter the Great Depression, which mangled the town's economy with a helping hand from the Mexican boll weevil, a beetle with an appetite for cotton crop destruction. Gruene's chance of survival was all but squashed until the 1970s saw a few Texans re-discover the area and bring music back to the cobwebbed dancehall there (after they convinced developers not to bulldoze). Slowly, business owners stepped in to take over historic buildings and Gruene was reborn.

Arrive in Gruene in the late afternoon and you'll have the perfect amount of time for dinner and a drink before checking out the dancehall. For those planning to spend the night, first check into your bed and breakfast at **Gruene Mansion Inn** (1275 Gruene Rd., 830/629-2641, www.gruenemansioninn.com). Right next door to Gruene Hall, the circa-1872 Victorian

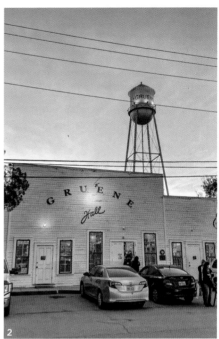

1: Gruene Antique Company **2:** Gruene Hall
3: Gruene General Store **4:** The Gristmill

inn has more than 30 rooms, each with its own porch. Clawfoot tubs and antiques are found throughout the B&B, and you'll be greeted with breakfast in the morning.

Head to **The Grapevine** (1612 Hunter Rd., 830/606-0093, www.grapevineingruene.com) for Texas wines, especially from Lubbock, and draft beers from around the state. On the weekends, take in live music from the porch or outdoor garden as you sip a Texas vino. Alternately, head over to **Winery on the Gruene** (1308 Gruene Rd., 830/608-1976, www.gruenewinery.com) where you can try a flight of four fruit-forward wines for $6, then buy a glass or bottle to enjoy on their patio.

For dinner, head towards the pansy-covered barrels next to Gruene Hall and walk down the stone path to **The Gristmill** (1287 Gruene Rd., 830/625-0684, http://gristmillrestaurant.com). In the shell of the 1878 three-story cotton-gin boiler room, take your pick of Texas comfort-food classics like fried catfish, chicken fried steak, or chicken fried chicken. A brick patio in an enchanting oak grove wrapped in string lights makes for a nice spot to wait for your table. For the best views, ask to dine on the multi-level back terrace overlooking the Guadalupe River.

After dinner, walk next door to **Gruene Hall** (1281 Gruene Rd., 830/606-1281, https://gruenehall.com). Built in 1878 by Henry D. Gruene, the Hall became known for parties that would pause at midnight for sandwiches and coffee breaks before rolling full speed ahead until 5am. The old polka and square-dancing hall also acted as a community center, hosting German singing festivals called Saengerfests and high school graduations. Performances at the Hall were instrumental Gruene's revival, billing singer-songwriters like George Strait, Lyle Lovett, and Willie Nelson. Music is still important to the Hall today, with live music played seven days a week, including daytime shows on Saturday and Sunday. Drop in to hear blues, Americana, and country-western.

While Gruene Hall no longer serves "dime a shot whiskey" as in the days of yore, you can grab a beer, wine, or sangria from the front bar. The Hall is cash only. All shows are all-ages, meaning you can bring your kids who will pay half-price, except for advance-ticketed weekend events (most weekday shows are free). Some shows are seated, some are standing, and some are dances, so call ahead if you have your heart set on one type or the other. The full calendar of events is on their website.

The crowd here is pure Texas, which is less like a caricature of a cowboy than you may

Celebrate

In New Braunfels, **Wurstfest** (https://wurstfest.com) has celebrated sausage since 1961. Based on the German festival Oktoberfest, Wurstfest offers tons of beer, food, and activities over 10 days. Accordions play, tubas oompah, and drinking songs abound starting on the last day in November. Liederhosen is encouraged, and there are more than 50 beers to sip between the craft beer gardens and mouthwatering food vendors.

imagine. Enjoy the low-fuss hall or boot scoot across the dance floor and onto the back patio to chat with your friends while the music washes over you from inside. Once you've had your fill, stroll over to your B&B for the night.

After breakfast, walk to **Gruene Coffee Haus** (1720 Hunter Rd., 830/625-5527, www.gruenecoffee.com) for a caffeine boost before checking out the shopping scene on Hunter Road. The **Gruene General Store** (1610 Hunter Rd., 830/629-6021, http://gruenegeneralstore.com) is the original mercantile store, built in 1878. Today, it sells a range of pickled items, fruit preserves, sauces, and ice cream floats. It was literally dragged across the street to its current location in 1904 to make room for the new mercantile shop, now **Gruene Antique Company** (1607 Hunter Rd., 830/629-7781, https://grueneantiqueco.com). The immaculate antique shop sells every manner of old item and is full of unexpected curiosities like glass eyeballs and rings of heavy skeleton keys.

With century-old stories and well-preserved architecture, Gruene is a remarkable piece of Texas' past well worth a visit.

Connect with . . .

38 Float the river in San Marcos

47 Drink with the devil at the Devil's Backbone Tavern

49 Explore a Texas jungle at Palmetto State Park

42 Sip your way through Texas Wine Country

Sip Something Strong • Day Trips

Why Go: Head to the Texas Hill Country to wander rows of dreamy sun-drenched grapevines, stopping to sip and swirl glasses of white and red along the way.

Where: Hill Country hosts an ever-growing number of wineries (50 and counting). THCW (Texas Hill Country Wineries) is an association of wineries throughout the AVA. For more information, visit www.texaswinetrail.com.

Timing: Plan on a relaxing evening at one winery or make a weekend of it, visiting three or four a day (with the support of a designated driver). Plan for each day to wrap up by 6pm.

On my first Texas Hill Country weekend, I discovered my new favorite wines—and learned the pronunciation of "tempranillo," the state's favored grape varietal. The number of wineries here means there are endless options to get acquainted with Lone Star vino. Tasting rooms are the perfect introduction to new bottles and new makers for novices and connoisseurs alike.

wine tasting at a vineyard

To begin your education in viticulture, simply pick a winery and order a tasting flight, consisting of four or five two-ounce pours, typically beginning with whites and ending with reds. Charcuterie boards that complement each wine's notes are sometimes available. If you like a particular wine, full glasses and bottles are of course easy to purchase.

If you're really committed to a wine adventure, join one of THCW's four signature **Passport Events:** the February Wine Lovers Celebration, the springtime Wine and Wildflower Journey, Texas Wine Month in October, or the Christmas Wine Affair. Over 40 wineries participate in each month-long event. A passport lets you visit up to four tasting rooms a day. Wine makers preselect tasting choices from their cellars, describing their flavors, aromas, and wine making techniques with each pour. It's a great

the patio at Ron Yates

enjoying the vineyards

founder Ron Yates with bartender Gabi

way to sample a variety of wineries and find the flavors for you. (Call ahead for hours; not every tasting room is open daily.)

My favorite section of the informal wine route is Highway 290 between Johnson City and Fredericksburg, which more than 25 wine makers call home. The drive from Austin is stunning. Vineyard crowds are very casual (signs in bathrooms advise guests to "not wash the mud off your shoes in the sink"). Designate a driver, a ride share, or a shuttle to get around. The 290 Wine Shuttle stops at 16 wineries in the Fredericksburg area for $40 (tastings not included).

I wistfully eyed their shiny, silver, 1978 airstream trailer and outdoor lights strung under an oak tree on my first visit to **Farmhouse Vineyard Marketplace and Tipsy Trailer** (402 E Main St., Johnson City, 806-752-7377, www.farmhousevineyard. com/Tipsy-The-Tasting-Trailer). The "marketplace" is a cozy house, decorated with candles, kettles, and wine glasses nestled neatly around rich blue and pink couches. Small bags of buttery popcorn are offered free, and I ordered a delicious panini to enjoy with my tasting. These wines, made from 100% Texas-grown grapes, named "Boyfriend" (a sparkling white) and "Cultivated" (a delicious red blend), represent the cream of the Farmhouse crop, or just 5% of the grapes they grow themselves. The rest of the grapes, grown in the southern Texas high plains outside Lubbock, are sold to the top 20 Texas wine makers.

The newer or smaller the tasting room, the more likely you are to meet the owner. I popped into **Ron Yates** (6676 Hwy 290 W, Hye, 512- 585-3972, www.ronyateswines.com) expecting to sip wine alone when gregarious owner Ron Yates himself appeared, greeting all with a warm handshake. Bearded, long-haired, and flip-flopped, Yates spoke of his lake upbringing, ranch-rooted family history, and wine-loving college days in Spain. Gabi, the friendly, outgoing bartender, shared her wine stories, too. She explained that the ubiquitous Texas tempranillo grape matures and is picked "early," dodging the brutal Texas summer. (The Spanish word "temprano," means early). Yates' full-bodied, deep red 2017 tempranillo won the coveted Houston Rodeo "Saddle" award. After one sip, I was sold.

Twenty miles down the road at the **Texas Wine Collective** (formerly 4.0 Cellars, 10354 E, 5761, US-290, Fredericksburg, 830-997-7470), some of the earliest Texas wine makers,

Celebrate

Held at Fair Market and Auditorium Shores in November, the **Austin Food & Wine Festival** (www.austinfoodandwinefestival.com) is foodie heaven, where local chefs are the angels. Tickets include a weekend of free-flowing libations, food samples, hands-on cooking demonstrations, music, and more. Highlights include the Rock Your Taco competition and eye-popping displays of unusual meats (think quail skewered on a tree branch).

McPherson, Lost Oak, and Brennan Vineyards, have collaborated on a modern tasting room. Vino pioneer Doc McPherson planted grapes in the 1970s after being caught secretly experimenting with wine making at the college where he taught chemistry. More recently, he won a Saddle for his 100% Texas grown 2017 Les Copains white wine. Other tasting standouts are McPherson's 2019 Chenin Blanc ("orange blossom on the nose and lemon meringue on the palette") and Brennan Vineyards' 2017 Austin Street Red ("dark chocolate covered strawberries on the nose and raspberry on the tongue").

No tour is complete without a stop at **Becker Vineyard** (464 Becker Farms Rd., Fredericksburg, 830- 644-2681, www.beckervineyards.com), where you'll find a stately reproduction of a 19th-century stone barn and delicious, approachable wine. Enjoy an all-white, all-red, or mixed tasting on The Verandah, near a big outdoor fireplace with tulips growing in the distance. I went home with a 2017 Viognier to uncork later with friends.

Connect with . . .

🅠 Get away to Fredericksburg

43 Get away to Fredericksburg

Getaway • Shopping • Taste of Texas • Sip Something Strong
• Hike & Bike • Scenic Drives • Best in Spring

Why Go: Nestled in the Hill Country, Fredericksburg blends natural beauty with 1800s charm. German restaurants, shopping, local wine, nearby hikes, and a scenic drive make this historic town the perfect weekend away.

Where: Fredericksburg (www.visitfredericksburgtx.com) • roughly 80 miles west of Austin

Timing: Spend two nights in Fredericksburg to eat, drink, and be merry. Spring is the best time to head out, as the Willow City Loop is unforgettable in full bloom.

Fredericksburg is a peach of an orchard-loving town. Founded in 1846, it offers a historic Main Street perfect for shopping, a lively restaurant scene reflecting the town's German roots, and plenty of wine tasting rooms. Nearby, the iconic Enchanted Rock, a dome of pink granite with a short, windy hike to its summit, is a must-see. In spring, Texas wildflowers grow in abundance along the stunning Willow City Loop scenic drive. All of which makes Fredericksburg a nest of Hill Country charm perfect for a weekend getaway.

Book a hotel stay at least two weeks in advance, since Fredericksburg can get busy during major holidays, local events, and in spring when the wildflowers are in bloom. Two of my favorites are **Hoffman Haus** (608 E Creek St., 830/997-6739, www.hoffmanhaus.com), a luxury B&B just off Main Street, and the collection of cottages at **The Blacksmith's Quarters on Baron's Creek** (417 E Main St., 830/998-1981, www.vacasa.com).

After checking in, make your way to the historic downtown. The six bustling blocks between Milam and Washington Streets are lined with mid-19th century fachwerk (a traditional German building style using timber and stone) buildings. Fashionable boutiques like **Remember Me, Too** (109 E Main St., 830/997-6444) are mingled with antique shops. **Headquarters Hats** (122 E Main St., 830/990-8510, www.headquartershats.com) offers custom western hats, boots, and Southwestern apparel. Those with a sweet tooth will want to

1: spaetzle at Auslander 2: Fredericksburg
3: wildflowers on the Willow City Loop
4: Enchanted Rock State Park

try one of the 35 flavors of homemade ice cream at **Clear River Ice Cream, Bakery & Deli** (138 E Main St., 830/997-8490, www.icecreamandfun.com). If want to learn more about the history of Fredericksburg, head to the **Pioneer Museum** (325 W Main St., 830/990-8441, www.pioneermuseum.net), where you can hear the history from the German immigrant's perspective and walk through original one-room schoolhouses, log cabins, smoke houses, and blacksmith workshops.

After, stop by a tasting room or two to sample some local Texas wines. **Becker Vineyards Main Street Tasting Room** (307 E Main St., 830/644-2681, www.beckervineyards.com) is a lovely, modern space. You can sample six wines on a covered outdoor patio. Be sure to try the staple of Texas reds: the oak-aged Tempranillo. A few blocks off Main Street, **Lost Draw Cellars** (113 E Park St., 830/992-3251, www.lostdrawcellars.com) has been owned by the same family since the 1930s. The five-pour tasting gives you a chance to sample Texas-grown high plains wines from Lubbock, including the super-popular Texas Tempranillo, a creamy white Roussanne, and a jammy Zinfandel. Afterwards, plan for dinner at one of the restaurants along Main Street.

Day two in Fredericksburg should start with breakfast and coffee. **Caliche Coffee** (338 W Main St., 830/992-3536, https://calichecoffee.com) serves delicious bagels with lox and breakfast burritos. For health nuts, **Frisch Juicerie** (The Peach Basket General Store, 334 W Main St., 830/534-1476, https://frisch-juicerie.business.site) next door offers hydrating smoothies and juices made from Fredericksburg peaches and other local fruits and vegetables.

Consider grabbing lunch to take on your excursion to **Enchanted Rock State Park** (16710 Ranch Rd. 965, 830/ 685-3636, https://tpwd.texas.gov), a 20-minute drive north. Don't forget your comfortable shoes, because you'll be climbing. The park's huge pink granite dome towers 1,825 feet, and the hike straight to the top of the dome is a moderately challenging climb. The roughly two-mile summit trail takes about an hour and half round trip, but you can stay as long as you like and explore the many miles of trails around the park, trekking past humongous boulders on Little Rock Trail and Echo Canyon Trail. You can reserve a day pass in advance on the park's website.

If you aren't too exhausted after your hike, head back to town for dinner at one of the iconic German restaurants. **Altdorf Biergarten** (301 W Main St., 830/997-7865, www.altdorfs.

Celebrate

Throughout the year, **Enchanted Rock State Park** hosts **"star parties,"** where you can gaze through expensive telescopes at the planets in our solar system. These events are especially spectacular here since Enchanted Rock is an International Dark Sky park. You can buy tickets on the park's website. Reserve well in advance for the night of a new moon when the sky is darkest. Nighttime howling by spirits of the rock, or potentially coyotes, is common.

com) and the **Auslander** (323 E Main St., 830/997-7714, https://theauslanderfredericksburg. com) both serve a variety of schnitzels, or thinly sliced fried cutlets. Try beer from Germany or brewed locally in Fredericksburg's own Alstadt. Both restaurants feature warm wood interiors and open-air patios. For a nightcap, head over to **Hondo's on Main** (312 W Main St., 830/997-1633, www.hondosonmain.com) for beer and a live band in their garden.

On your way back home, be sure to make a detour to drive the stunning **Willow City Loop,** a 13-mile scenic drive half an hour northeast of Fredericksburg. During wildflower season, April through early May, bluebonnets blanket the hills, and the landscape is sprinkled with red Indian paintbrushes, violet phlox, sunshine yellow coreopsis, and Mexican poppies. To get there, head towards North State Highway 16 and make a right on Farm Road 1323 until you hit Willow City Loop, then take a left and follow the road slowly around and back up to Highway 16. As one Fredericksburg resident said, the loop "looks like a lake with all the bluebonnets." Drive slowly, watching out for the cattle that roam freely. Take a moment to gaze across the open valley farms and pull over for a few photos before making your way back to Austin.

Connect with . . .

42 Sip your way through Texas Wine Country

44 Take a dip in Hamilton Pool

Outdoor Adventures • Get on the Water • Day Trips • Family Friendly

Why Go: A breathtaking Hill Country swimming hole capped off with sweet, tart beer and wood-fired, Neapolitan-style pizza make for the perfect Texas day.

Where: A half an hour west of Austin, Dripping Springs is home to Hamilton Pool (24300 Hamilton Rd., Dripping Springs, 512/264-2740, https://parks.traviscountytx. gov). On your way home, stop by Jester King Brewery (13187 Fitzhugh Rd., Austin, 512/661-8736, https://jesterkingbrewery.com).

Timing: Half-day reservations for Hamilton Pool are just the right amount of time to swim and relax before heading out for pizza and brews. Summertime is best for maximum greenery and oasis enjoyment. Winter waterflow is more of a trickle, with the pool temperature dipping below 50 degrees Fahrenheit.

Tucked away in secluded canyon, **Hamilton Pool** is the VIP area of Austin water recreation. The large, shaded pool is framed by a limestone outcropping overhead and a deep rock bowl behind a beautiful 50-foot waterfall. Golden cheeked warblers, snapping turtles, and fish are at home with riparian flora like the exotic chatterbox orchid. Walk along the pebble-covered shore for natural rock exfoliation or lay out on the hot stones for a body weight massage and a tan. Jump in the pool to cool off, alternating between lazing in the shallow area or losing yourself in 25-foot-deep dives. Photos are de rigueur.

Not surprisingly, given the popularity of such a luxurious natural space, reservations need to be made in advance. Reservations are divided into half-day slots, with the morning one running from 9am until 1pm and the afternoon from 2pm until 6pm. In 2018, Austin's NPR station reported that demand was so high that scalpers were selling tickets for $50. Normally, tickets are much more affordable: $12 per car online and then an additional $8 per person; cash only, when you arrive at the gate. The person who booked the reservation should bring their photo ID. After you've made your reservation, check ahead to make sure that swimming will still be allowed that day. Sometimes the pool is restricted if there is a high bacteria count. You can reschedule a reservation any time before midnight the day before your planned visit.

Hamilton Pool

relaxing in the waterfall

Bring comfortable, grippy shoes for the steep descent to the pool area. If you're getting into the water, you might bring a second pair of shoes too, or at least a pair you don't mind swimming in. Rocks in the pool sometimes make water shoes the most comfortable bet, but plenty of people wear foam sandals on their sensitive dogs, too. (Real dogs are not allowed. Sorry.) Bring a thick towel for drying off and padding your seat on the rocky and pebbly shore. Folding chairs, food, and drinks are allowed in the park, but no glass. Life jackets are available to everyone.

After your time at the pool, take a 15-minute drive south to **Jester King Brewery** in Dripping Springs for lunch or dinner. Using yeast found on their land for fermentation, Jester King makes delicious farmhouse ales which translate to some truly tart, juicy, memorable beers, often incorporating interesting Texas fruit like the new Barrel Aged Wild Ale with Jambolan plums. It's an acquired taste, but many of my friends can't get enough of this fizzy, fruity refreshment. Try a flight to get acquainted with a diverse range, like the Figlet, a farmhouse ale made with smoked figs in collaboration with Franklin Barbecue, or the Spon, a Belgian lambic.

Hamilton Pool in springtime

Wood-fired Neapolitan style pizza is the main food option. (Saving your appetite for a pizza after a Hill Country swim means that you don't have to worry about swimming cramps due to poolside snacking.) Try one of the unique creations, like the vegan Cali pizza with spicy black bean sauce and avocado puree. They are also branching out into smoked meats and barbecue. Eat at one of the picnic tables set all around the 165-acre property. After you eat, wander around the working farm cooing at the bunnies and baby goats.

By now you've been immersed in Hill Country water and drunk of its alcohol. The Hill Country tastes sweet and a little strange. Are you a fan?

Connect with . . .

⓴ Drink ancient desert spirits

㊿ Sip liquid sunshine on the Texas Whiskey Trail

45 Find every waterfall at Colorado Bend State Park

Outdoor Adventures • Hike & Bike • Get on the Water • Day Trips

Why Go: Waterfalls are a special sight in Texas, and these falls, surrounded by emerald moss and ferns, are exceptionally beautiful.

Where: Colorado Bend State Park • 2236 Park Hill Dr., Bend • 325/628-3240 • https://tpwd.texas.gov

Timing: The waterfalls are spectacular in the summer, when everything is lush and green, but it's also when the heat is at its worst. Plan to arrive extra early and hike in the cooler morning air. You can also visit in late spring or early fall when things aren't quite as green, but the weather is perfect.

Two hours northwest of Austin, oaks, elms, and pecan trees meet the Edwards Plateau, creating an oasis where hikers can hunt for waterfalls across 5,000 acres of Hill Country beauty. The

▲ scenic overlook

waterfalls at Colorado Bend State Park have been compared to those in Costa Rica and Hawaii, which is a surprise considering the hot, dry state of Texas is more known for ranches and pine trees than crystal cascades. At over 60-feet tall, Gorman Falls is the most well-known waterfall inside the park, but a handful of smaller, hidden gems are absolutely also worth seeking out.

Reserve your $5 day-use pass for the park online well before you arrive. Weekends are busy, especially during summer, so book your pass a few weeks out. Weekdays are less crowded and walk-up passes are often available then. In the summertime, start your trek early in the morning, as Texas temperatures climb dangerously high. The trail to the main waterfall is mostly unshaded, and 100-degree weather is dehydrating even for native Texans. The standard recommended water allowance is one liter per mile hiked per person. Grippy, comfortable shoes are a must on the rocky trails, especially the slippery trail down to Gorman Falls. Pets are allowed but must be leashed.

1: swimming in Spicewood Springs **2:** Gorman Falls **3:** the trail to Gorman Falls **4:** Bend General Store

See all the waterfalls at Colorado Bend, starting with the smallest, dotting Spicewood Springs Trail, and ending with the biggest, on Gorman Falls Trail. Three miles round-trip and rising 300 feet in elevation, **Spicewood Springs Trail** is a challenging but rewarding out-and-back. The namesake spring is perfect for idyllic creek and small-waterfall crossings and offers a cool natural pool to jump into before the trail starts climbing north. Swimming is allowed in the spring and summer. To get to the trailhead, park by the river group camping site at the southeast end of the park, west of the park headquarters, and follow the Spicewood Canyon Trail for a short bit as it parallels the Colorado River. When the trail forks, go left. For something more challenging, go right at the fork to stay on **Spicewood Canyon Trail.** A 6-mile out-and-back, this trail has waterfalls only a few feet high but no less stunning. Creek crossings and the chance to dip your feet in are refreshing and rejuvenating. Keep your eyes open for cool Texas bugs, like the giant red-headed centipede, and families of deer leaping through the woods.

Located at the end of a rocky trail worn down by countless nature lovers, Gorman Falls

▲ the Colorado River at Colorado Bend State Park

looks like something from a fantasy quest. To access **Gorman Falls Trail,** park in the lot by the park's entrance, where you'll see trailheads for Gorman Falls and Tie Slide Trails. The majority of the 3-mile (round-trip) hike is rocky, unshaded, and flat until the end when you reach the steep, slippery descent down the falls. It can be a challenging hike, but when you're sitting on the small landing in the misty air taking in the falls, it'll feel worth it. Gorman Falls runs year-round, and unlike most waterfalls, it grows each year thanks to a buildup of limestone deposits. The deposits are delicate, so no one is allowed to stand near the waterfall, but the view is spectacular.

For a really unique waterfall experience, rent a kayak and paddle down the sunny Colorado River to **Post Oak Falls.** While the cascade is smaller than Gorman, it's only accessible by boat, making it exceptionally rare. Rent a single or double kayak from the park($10-$15/hour) and park by the South Camping Area to begin the trip. The falls will emerge on your left-hand side about two miles past the park boundary. Falls flow down tiers of mossy green rock like a cake, mostly in the summer, dependent on rain. Be ready for a strenuous upper body workout as you paddle out and back to enjoy this hidden beauty.

While waterfalls are the main event, Colorado Bend State Park is no one-trick pony. Swimming, fishing, and camping opportunities abound. Birders should bring binoculars for a chance to see nearly 200 bird species through their magnifying goggles. Caving adventures range from comfortable strolls to claustrophobic crawls. Regardless of how you spend your day, dinner at **Bend General Store** (112 County Road 438, Bend, 325/628-3523), 3.5 miles outside the park entrance, will hit the spot. They serve up southern classics and host live music on the weekends.

46 Step back in time at Dinosaur Park

Family Friendly

Why Go: Dinosaur Park is a fun, inexpensive, educational journey to see life-size dinosaurs in an outdoor park.

Where: Dinosaur Park • 893 Union Chapel Road, Cedar Creek • 512/321-6262 • www.thedinopark.com

Timing: Dinosaur spotting is a weekend sport, with the park open Thursday to Sunday from 10am to 4pm. Plan to spend about an hour and keep in mind that you have to hit the trail by 3:30pm at the latest. Reservations are not necessary.

I knew I loved Dinosaur Park when I met Sue. She is no mere skeleton, standing 60 feet tall and 40 feet long, towering in forest green with fearsome teeth and improbably tiny arms.

▲ triceratops

Sue is a model of an original T. rex specimen on display at the Field Museum in Chicago. She is far from the only prehistoric model in Texas, thanks to Dinosaur Park, an ever-expanding outdoor museum with a half mile-trail and over 30 models of life-size dinosaurs. Dinos range in size from a massive, long-necked Brachiosaurus to the turkey-sized Compsognathus. For any curious paleontologists, Dinosaur Park's focus is the Cretaceous period but includes a few animals from the Triassic, Jurassic, and Micoene, too.

The park is an inexpensive family date, with affordable tickets, free parking, and the option to bring your own picnic. Small pets are allowed on a leash, and you can rent a wagon for a dollar, which makes navigating the flat but unpaved trail easier. Plan to spend 30 minutes to an hour on the dinosaur path, but you can snag a picnic table and head to the playground if you want to stay longer. You can buy tickets inside the gift shop while surrounded by oodles of colorful dinosaur-themed toys.

Your absorbing road to prehistoric times begins between two Sauropods to the left of the playground behind the gift shop. Progress at your own pace along a winding walking safari

▲ stegosaurus

▲ the great T-Rex

▲ brachiosaurus

as dinosaurs of every size appear among the trees. Each herbivore, carnivore, and omnivore has a dedicated, educational sign documenting the animal's scientific name, nickname, height, weight, length, location, and time period, among other cool details. Did you know the hulking Stegosaurus, with impressive plates standing along its back and tail, had a brain the size of a walnut? And that it's speculated it had a "second brain" near its hip? An important nerve bundle 20x the size of a walnut was discovered above the Stegosaurus' hind legs and scientists are still disputing possible uses.

Every turn along the trail reveals another oddly shaped predator or gentle giant. The herbivorous Parasaurolophus sports a pretty blue bone plate on its head, which scientists believe made a loud sound and was used for communication. This crest is slim when compared to the giant domed skull of the Stegoceras. The Iguanodon, star of Disney's movie *Dinosaur,* and the Velociraptor, of *Jurassic Park* infamy, are here too.

A few non-dinosaurs appear on the trail, like Megalania, the 23-foot-long lizard, and Kelenken, the apex predator known as "Terror Bird" that lived well after the dinosaurs went extinct. Short explanations teach ways to identify what was *not* a dinosaur. Could it fly? How were its legs positioned? Following the "scavenger hunt" of questions posted every few yards will keep both kids and adults engaged. Can you spot the coprolite (dinosaur poop) and the dinosaur tracks hidden among the trees? How about the Coelurosauravus, a flying lizard whose name means "Hollow Lizard Grandfather"?

A note of caution: Homo sapiens are not allowed behind the small, draped chain in front of each dinosaur exhibit, but the tiny dinosaurs with little saddles on them, called "Picture Pals," are fair game. The whole family can pile into the humongous dinosaur nest with white eggs or pose under the upright jawbone of a Mastodon. For the other displays, like the amazing Diplodocus, which stands 18-20 feet high and 100-120 feet long, pictures can be taken from a safe distance only.

The end of your half-mile trail delivers you safely back to the playground area. Wiggle worms can ride the little purple and green dinosaurs here, as well as swing and slide to their hearts content. Across the playground, a few sandboxes are set up as shaded Dino Digs, where budding paleontologists can kneel over buried "fossils" and practice field work.

I visited Dinosaur Park alone, but I'm far from the only adult beckoned by these great beings that once ruled the planet. The owners attest to the intriguing power of dinosaur facts, having built the park in 2005 after their entire family was pulled into dinosaur appreciation by their young son. As I left, still in dinosaur mode, I heard the Carolina chickadees chirping nearby. Chickadees can fly, so they are not dinosaurs, I recited in my head, still thinking of the somewhat bizarre, incredibly large, flightless "Terror Bird."

Connect with . . .

48 Fly through the trees at Zip Lost Pines

47 Drink with the devil at the Devil's Backbone Tavern

Nightlife • Sip Something Strong

Why Go: Keep an eye out for ghosts as you grab a drink at this charming old Texas haunt.

Where: Devil's Backbone Tavern • 4041 Farm to Market 32, Fischer • 830/964-2544 • www.devilsbackbonetavern.com

Timing: The tavern is open from noon until 10pm on weekdays, and from noon until midnight on weekends. Bring cash for the cash-only bar. The tavern is roughly 45 miles outside of Austin; drive during the daytime when you can see the views.

Under a yellow billboard with the Devil staring down at me, Mickey Gilley piped in on outdoor speakers singing about heartache. My date was a half hour late to the Devil's Backbone Tavern, so I went in alone and ordered a Devil's Backbone beer (made at nearby Real Ale Brewery) from a nice bartender who called me baby and told me nobody drinks that here. A group of white-haired men in the corner all chimed in to agree before they went out the back door, Bud Lights in hand, to sit in the sun. "Isn't this place haunted?" I asked. The bartender nodded, and the last man inside said he'd definitely seen some things through the years, before heading out to join his friends.

Ominously named, the Devil's Backbone Tavern lies on the limestone ridge running between San Marcos and Blanco. The Sunday-drive crowd will love the hilly views. Once you get to San Marcos, get on Ranch Road 12 and drive 10 miles to Farm to Market Road 32. Make a left and in four miles, notice the rolling hills spread out to both sides of your car. Just as the view starts, the Devil's Backbone Tavern appears to your left. Friendly regulars and ghost stories in this 1930s honky-tonk make it a great stop or date rendezvous, even if your date never shows up. Park free in front of or behind the bar.

The tavern is a dive-bar dream. The long, squat limestone-walled building dates back to the late 1800s. Nowadays its ceiling is papered in dollar bills and the whole place feels comfortably unpretentious with worn wood floors sandy from the shuffle ball table. Patio tables are

view from the Devil's Backbone

planted around a fire pit out back, beneath the oak trees and string lights. Red and yellow tinsel draped over the dancehall at 2pm on a quiet weekday when I stopped in.

Live music is a staple at the Tavern on weekends. Rock, country, and folk musicians regularly rotate through, and singer-songwriters like Sarah Jaffe and Susan Tedeschi will drop in. The only time I saw a man two-step with two women at once was to a rollicking fiddle-fronted set from Austin's Warren Hood. For other times, a jukebox at the far end of the bar is a treasure trove of country and western with albums from Gary P. Nunn, The Chicks, and Charley Pride. Thursdays are jam night when anyone can bring an instrument and join with other players in a communal open-mic session.

People at the Tavern are as welcoming as Psycho the black cat, the friendly feline allowed to prowl inside the bar. When I visited, bar-goers included everyone within earshot in their conversations and shook hands graciously. "You should come back Saturday for the big birthday party," one said. A communal birthday party for anyone born that month happens on Sec-

▲ Devil's Backbone Tavern

ond Saturdays, and all are invited. Regulars and bartenders even indulged me in a few ghost stories when I asked. The entire Devil's Backbone ridge is said to be haunted.

"We had people from New York in here with all kinds of gadgets looking for ghosts," explained Charlie Beatty, a longtime bar-goer. Ghost hunters told Beatty that the ghosts really liked him. He also told how photos of deceased patrons hung on the walls would sometimes fall when widows came by speaking ill of their misbehaved late husbands. Eventually the bar had to stop putting the pictures back up. The bartender told a story about turning off all the inside lights, one-by-one, and then seeing them all light back up inexplicably.

The whole Devil's Backbone area is full of ghost stories, although apparently ghost activity had been low as of late. There are whispers of wolf spirits possessing travelers who crossed the area. Other stories talk of phantom stampedes rattling quiet homes nearby.

I've been to the tavern plenty of times and never been possessed, but maybe I didn't have the right attitude. No one I know has been possessed either. Then again, maybe waiting two hours for a date is a little eerie.

48 Fly through the trees at Zip Lost Pines

Outdoor Adventures • Family Friendly

Why Go: Get a rush zip lining over the treetops with a flying birds-eye view of McKinney Roughs Nature Park.

Where: Zip Lost Pines • McKinney Roughs Nature Park, 1760 State Highway 71 W, Cedar Creek • 512/761-2323 • https://ziplostpines.com

Timing: Check-in, suit up, zip down, and arrive safely back at your car in 2-3 hours for the full six-line course, which runs earlier in the day with the first launch starting at 9am. The half course takes 1-2 hours and runs in the afternoon, between noon and 4:30pm. The night tour, also 1-2 hours, only runs on Friday and Saturday evenings at 8pm and 8:30pm. The park is closed Tuesday and Wednesday. Tours may be rescheduled due to bad weather.

Like a spy in a high-tech novel, the instructor leaned back, tucked her legs tight into her chest and floated away over the trees, receding into the morning fog without a word. My turn came next. Suspended from a harness by a few heavy straps and some solid pieces of metal, I sat down low, lifted my feet, and slid down a thousand feet of wire.

Located in McKinney Roughs Nature Park, half an hour east of Austin, Zip Lost Pines offers a bird's-eye view of Texas. Sail across zip lines at 15 to 30 miles per hour, curling up like a ball to gain speed or stretching your arms and legs out like a starfish to slow down. Feel free to yell and twirl. I constantly slid down the line backwards, facing the launch platform with the grace of a hooked worm, but your zip-line style will be unique. Below you, cacti, loblolly pine, and oaks rush by. And if you pay attention on a clear day, you can see the Colorado River.

The **Full Zip Line Tour** includes rides on six zip lines over nearly a mile through the canopy for $115. Tours that launch earlier in the morning avoid the hottest hours of the hellacious Texas summer. The **Half Zip Line Tour** for $95 includes three zip lines to introduce the ride to newbies. On Friday and Saturday, the **Night Zip Line Tour** for $105 is the same as a half-tour but with twinkling stars and glowing harnesses and platforms. Time a night zip to

▲ the rope bridge at Zip Lost Pines

▲ zipliners flying overhead

▲ Zip Lost Pines

coincide with a full moon for the best visibility. For all tours, zippers go down the lines in pairs, riding side-by-side on parallel lines, but single riders can fly, too.

Safety is a top priority at Lost Pines. The instructors run the entire course every day before visitors arrive as a safety check. While there is no age limit for riders, weight requirements are firm: you must weigh-in at 50 to 250 pounds, and you'll step on a scale at check-in to prove it. Staff help visitors properly don thick, strappy black harnesses, tightening, fastening, and clamping for the best fit. Helmets are checked before every line, too.

The first line, Piney Plunge, is the shortest at only 146 feet. With speeds of 10 to 15 miles per hour, this leisurely soar over the flat Texas Blackland Prairie makes for a good warm up. Once acclimated to the mechanical whir of zip lines and the rush of sliding like a bead on a thread, the Cactus Corridor line ups the ante with speeds of up to 30 mph over 672 feet. Each zip line is a short hike away from the next. Along the way, you'll climb beautiful spiraling staircases to reach the platforms and cross wobbly but secure wood and rope suspension bridges. Heads up: friends might see this as an opportunity to challenge your balance by jumping and

▲ midair at Zip Lost Pines

stomping on them as you try to cross. Keep an eye out for the little details while you soak up the views. Take line four, Loblolly Land, for instance. When taking in the views of the Colorado River, you might miss the eagles. Bald eagles have built huge, eight-by-six foot heavy nests in a pecan tree visible from the top of the line. Each line ends with a jolting breaking system at the opposite platform, where guides wait to pull you in, hook you safely down, and then ask you to step aside while they reel in the rest of your party.

Lines four and six, the ones named for Loblolly Pine and River Run are the longest, at 1074 and 1316 feet respectively. The runs offer nice views of the blackjack oaks, post oaks, and loblolly pines spreading out in the 1440-acre park. A few streams and creeks wind below your ride, including the flowing Colorado River to the north. Guides are generous helpers, taking photos of you and your buddies overlooking the foliage below. Our guides even went so far as to help people pose, using step stools as props and offering tips on where to get an eye-catching background. Everyone rides back in a van at the end of the course after carefully shimmying out of zip equipment and regaining balance. Yours truly was left only a little dizzy.

Connect with . . .

46 Step back in time at Dinosaur Park

49 Explore a Texas jungle in Palmetto State Park

Outdoor Adventures • Hike & Bike • Day Trips

Why Go: An extraordinary, lush jungle landscape thrives at Palmetto State Park just a few miles away from legendary Texas history.

Where: Palmetto State Park • 78 Park Road 11 South, Gonzales • 830/672-3266 • tpwd.texas.gov/state-parks/palmetto

Timing: Palmetto State Park is open daily from 8:15am-4:45pm. You'll want to start your day early, so you have time to hit a few trails before venturing to Gonzales to visit the museums. Summer is an especially great time to visit, perfect for jumping into the park's Oxbow Lake or San Marcos River.

Jungle scenes are unheard of here. Central Texas is shrubby grassland country with rolling hills out west, but Palmetto State Park in Gonzales, an hour and 15 minutes southeast of Austin, looks a lot like Jurassic Park. Green dwarf palmettos thrive in the humid terrain, Spanish moss hangs down from tree limbs, and swamps dot the lush tropical landscape. Take a hike, bring a picnic, and enjoy this unique Texas land. You can easily make a day out of it by traveling just 12 miles into downtown Gonzales, the legendary city that started the Texas Revolution.

▲ dwarf palmettos

At Palmetto State Park, dwarf palmettos reign supreme among the 500 different types of plant life. Like palm trees with the trunk knocked out from beneath them, dwarf palmettos are tropical fronds. Five to 10 feet high with fanned, pointed tips, the palmettos blanket more than 20 green acres, growing thickly along the many flat, short hiking trails. Try the **Ottine Swamp Trail** to try to find the rumored Ottine Swamp Thing, a local bigfoot. If you're brave, check out the **Canebrake Spur Trail** and keep your eyes open for the timber rattlesnakes. To hike near larger bodies of water than the swamps, try the **Oxbow Lake Trail** or **San Marcos River Trail.** Most trails are less than a mile long, making it easy to do a handful in one day.

Amid the swamps and woods and sandy riverbanks, try to spot flying squirrels and Eastern narrow-mouthed toads. American trumpet creepers bloom in long cone shapes from vines high overhead. Grey-green Spanish moss drapes gently from above. Round little ruby-crowned kinglets with stunning crimson mullets and highlighter-yellow Prothonotary Warblers flit around. Swamps periodically drain and fill along the Ottine Swamp Trail, making them ephemeral but important parts of sustaining diverse life in Palmetto. After hiking, stop for a quick lunch at a picnic table near the big pavilion in the center of the park.

Daily entrance fees are $3 per person. You don't need a reservation for weekdays, but weekends can get busy. Reserve online or by phone a few days in advance to make sure you'll get in. To camp, you'll need to reserve at least two months ahead for spring and summer weekends.

While you're in the area, history buffs will want to make the 12-mile drive to the nearby town of Gonzales to visit the impressive Old County Jail Museum and the Gonzales Memorial Museum. A circa-1887 three-story structure, the **Gonzales County Jail Museum** (414 St Lawrence St., 830/263-4663) offers tours for only $2 every half hour Wednesday-Sunday. Iron bars, a dungeon-like vault, and a two-story replica of the gallows make for a chilling scene. In 1901, an inmate escaped the jail by pretending to be part of the tours that bustled in to see the famous folk hero and outlaw Gregorio Cortez. The free **Gonzales Memorial Museum** (414 Smith St., 830-672-6350) houses the original "Come and Take It" cannon. This cannon was given to Gonzales by Mexico to help defend against attacks, but when Mexico wanted it back, Gonzales was defiant and residents fired it at Mexican soldiers, thus firing the first shots of the Texas Revolution. Hours vary for both museums; call ahead or visit www.gonzalestexas.com/museums.

A full day in Gonzales is a surprising juxtaposition of experiences. Botanical forested wetlands and bog-like views of dwarf palmettos as far as the eye can see at Palmetto State Park are a standout among any Texas landscape. The heavily significant history in the same city is also striking, surrounded by beautiful, centuries old homes and families with deep roots in the area. The area is one you will want to return to again and again.

50 Sip liquid sunshine on the Texas Whiskey Trail

Sip Something Strong

Why Go: A relative newcomer on the whiskey scene, Texas distilleries grew fast and proud, standing up to the best on the planet with a swaggering spirit.

Where: There are distilleries throughout Austin and the Hill Country, with a concentration in Blanco. To learn more visit https://texaswhiskeytrail.com.

Timing: The best way to experience the Texas Whiskey Trail is by savoring slowly. Pick one distillery you'd like to learn more about and head over in the afternoon with friends. After a distillery tour, sip a cocktail or a whiskey neat in the tasting room.

Texas Whiskey Trail's brochure makes no mention, but the underdog Texas spirit that won a blind taste-test against the best whiskeys in the world is on their map. A distiller inspired by the criminal poisoning of a majestic 600-year-old oak in Austin is there, too, as is a distiller hanging raw, wild boar inside the still. Texas whiskey is rooted in the land. Grain-to-glass spirits are the pride of distillers, meaning they don't source pre-made whiskey; they process and age it right here in the Lone Star State. Not that there's anything wrong with doing it different, but Texas-made should mean just that.

▲ Treaty Oak Distilling

The Texas Whiskey Trail is comprised of distilleries all throughout Texas, but those in Austin and the Hill Country will knock your boots off. Use the online trail map as a guide and take a designated driver or ride share. A $75 Trail Pass buys a tasting at all Trail Member locations. In general, distilleries are not near one another except in the case of "the Blanco hat trick" where three distilleries are huddled together in the town of Blanco an hour west of Austin. Reserve tours ahead of time. They last around 45 minutes and are usually available on weekday evenings and more frequently on weekends. Some distilleries also hit it out of the park with great food on premises.

South Austin's **Still Austin Whiskey Co.** (440 E St. Elmo Rd., Ste. F, Austin,

1: bottles at Treaty Oak Distilling **2:** Andalusia Whiskey Co. **3:** Milam & Greene bourbon **4:** bar at Milam & Green Whiskey

▲ Real Ale Brewing
Co.'s spirit barrels

512/276-2700, https://stillaustin.com) has an unforgettable tour complete with a guided tasting. Tour and Education Manager Josh Madere was a font of whiskey lore. Did you know that a horizontal line drawn across Europe separates the cold northern barley-growing, whiskey-producing regions from the sunny southern grape and wine producing areas? That the first distiller was an Arabic woman named Mary? Our guide went a step beyond teaching us how whiskey is made and let us smell and interact with different stages of production. Don't miss Still's flagship grain-to-glass bourbon, The Musician. Try a twist on the classic old fashioned (they add Aztec chocolate bitters) on the artfully landscaped patio or around shared tables in the communal tasting room.

Named for a famous old oak tree in Austin, **Treaty Oak Distilling** (16604 Fitzhugh Rd., Dripping Springs, 512/400-4023, www.treatyoakdistilling.com) pours three tasters in a rustic, welcoming distillery. On the tour, my guide explained how temperature changes force barrels to "breathe," causing quick evaporation; 20% of a cask's contents can evaporate in one Texas year, compared to 10% in Kentucky and 2% in Scotland. That means sweet barrel flavors impart quickly in the non-climate controlled rickhouse (aging warehouse). My favorite whiskey was the Day Drinker bourbon, with both sweet and spicy notes. Grab a cocktail to sip on the huge lawn outside while live bands play or have lunch at Alice's Restaurant, a barbecue joint named after the Treaty Oak founder's mother.

Smoked in a Tuff Shed behind the tasting room, barley is the only ingredient in **Andalusia Whiskey Co.'s** (6462 US-281, Blanco, 830/507-4359, www.andalusiawhiskey. com) whiskey. Varied mash bills (recipes) produce six different whiskeys, each with their own roast and smoke profiles. Stryker, "barbecue in a bottle," draws its aromatic smoke profile from oak, mesquite, and applewood, while Bottled in Bond has "a heavy barrel character" and tastes medicinal. Founder Tommy Erwin suggests adding a straw-full of water to the glass when you taste to "bloom the whiskey," which dampens the strong alcohol taste and helps the other flavors shine. Andalusia white whiskey drinks like a tequila and goes well in a margarita or horchata. Tried too many whiskeys and can no longer taste the difference? Tommy says to breathe into the crook of your elbow to reset your palette.

Milam & Greene Whiskey's (208 Carlie Ln., Blanco, 830/833-3033, https://milamandgreenewhiskey.com) master distiller, Marlene Holmes, graciously let me taste the mash from a glass dipped straight into the mashton. "It tastes like cereal, doesn't it?" she asks. Marlene's 27 years of experience at Jim Beam, combined with master blender Heather Greene's brains make the outfit confident and creative. Double distilled, Milam & Greene whiskey goes into the bottle at 110 proof, a bit lower than it has to, so that more flavor is pronounced in the glass. While Milam & Greene does produce some grain-to-glass whiskey, they also experiment with aging whiskey in other states to create fantastic, spicy blends.

Brad Farbstein, founder of **Real Ale Brewing Co.** (231 San Saba Ct., Blanco, 830/833-2534, https://realalebrewing.com) touts unique yeast at this brewery and distillery. Real Ale Straight Malt Whiskey is my favorite, a slightly aggressive, spicy spirit. The Totem, however, has the story you'll remember. A malted barley, wheat, and passion fruit base, Totem is inspired by a rustic Oaxacan mezcal-based spirit, pechuga. Pechuga traditionally uses a raw chicken or turkey breast, but at Real Ale, rendered fat from a cold-smoked raw wild boar drips into the distillate, imparting "oily richness." Sip your bronze spirits on Real Ale's outdoor patio beneath shady trees, where you can listen to live music on weekends.

Connect with . . .

40 Drink ancient desert spirits
42 Sip your way through Texas Wine Country

51 Drive through the "Swiss Alps of Texas"
on the Twisted Sisters

Scenic Drives • Day Trips • Getaway

Why Go: These undeveloped Hill Country roads are a scenic desert loop of canyons, curves, and coils. Steep cliffs and stunning views make the route unforgettable.

Where: An hour northwest from San Antonio or two hours southwest of Austin, this stunning panoramic drive starts in Medina and heads west on Ranch Road 337 to Leakey. From Leakey, it makes a rectangular loop using Ranch Road 336, TX 41, Ranch Road 335, and Ranch Road 337. It then heads back east from Leakey to Medina.

Timing: The drive itself takes about 3 hours, but if you're coming from Austin, this is an all-day excursion, and you'll need to start early in the morning to make it back to the city by dark, even in summer when the days are long. It's more doable from San Antonio. Otherwise, rent a small-town cabin and do some stargazing miles away from the light-polluted cities.

In the Hill Country, the Twisted Sisters are not just a hair metal band from the '80s. Drooled over by motorcycle riders, this drive is known as one of the best scenic routes in America. Wild, dangerous curves run unimpeded and bold for over 100 miles. Called the Swiss Alps of Texas, this sequence of highway is hilly and majestic. It's well-traveled, but remote. Need to clear your mind? This drive is perfect. Prep your playlist, grab your sunglasses, and gas up the car. Let's roll.

You've got four long, undulating roads to tackle. The trip starts two hours southwest of Austin and takes three hours to drive in a rectangle of swinging turns and tight corners, then two hours to get back to Austin. You start in Medina, head west on RR 337 to Leakey, and then you drive the rectangular loop. Drive the rectangle counterclockwise to follow conventional wisdom on optimal views: Head north on RR 336, west on TX 41, and south on RR 335 back to Camp Wood. (If you want to be a rebel, drive the rectangle clockwise instead.) From Camp Wood, you head east on RR 337, through Leakey and back to Medina. Gas stations are sparse along this route; the only three places to gas up are Medina, Vanderpool, and Leakey.

It's easy to get caught up in the drive, but you should take it slow on the winding two-lane roads. Those speed limits are the law for a good reason. There's no shoulder for most of this drive and roads get rough and unpredictable at times. Yours truly spun out making a U-turn at the southeast corner of the route trying to drive it alone for the first time. Keep your eyes on the road and watch for darting animals.

Start your drive in **Medina.** Head west on **Ranch Road 337** (RR 337) for 20 miles until you reach **Vanderpool,** where you'll "T" into Market Road 187. A quick detour a few miles north on Market Road 187 takes you to the **Lone Star Motorcycle Museum** (36517 RM 187, https://lonestarmotorcyclemuseum.com), a great place to stretch your legs. You can check out vintage bikes, rare road racers from the 1910s, suicide clutches, and antique Triumphs like the one Marlon Brando rode in *The Wild One*. Once you've had your fill, head back south on Market Road 187 for 3 miles and turn right onto RR 337. You'll hit your first stretch of twisty turns just past Vanderpool. RR 337 offers some of the most romantic movie-scene vistas you'll drive in Texas. Enjoy the vast ranch land stretching for miles in either direction as you continue for 16.4 miles until you get to **Leakey.**

▲ Ranch Road 337

▲ rural Camp Wood

For the next leg of the drive, head north on US-83 for about a mile and then turn left (west) onto **Ranch Road 336** (RR 336). Drive 27 miles up RR 336 to the northeast corner of the rectangle, hugging the West Frio River. The drive climbs up, passing through intermittent canyon walls, and offers wide views of tumbling hills. Slower driving is rewarded on these tight turns, especially since you'll likely be sharing the road with motorcyclists and potential animal crossings. Slowing down will also give you time to take in the vast, rolling views.

RR 336 T's into **Texas 41,** where you take a left and drive 13 miles over to the northwest corner of the Texas Twisted Sisters rectangle. More of a helpful step-sister, this ranch road is a relatively straight (and not as scenic) connecting piece of the trip.

Hang another left onto **Ranch Road 335** (RR 335). Hackberry Creek ambles by, and you'll skirt and cross the Nueces River, past ranches and gently sprawling hills. For 29 miles, enjoy the rollercoaster road and switchbacks as the wind sweeps against your windows, until you come to the tiny town of **Camp Wood.**

Here, you'll head east on **RR 337,** the final leg of the drive. Sometimes described as the best part of the entire trip, this leg features deep valleys cut by the Frio and Nueces Rivers through the area. It's 58 miles from Camp Wood all the way to Medina.

There are a few nearby **accommodations** if you'd like to spend the night before trekking back to Austin. In Camp Wood, there's **Now & Then Cottage** (308 Frio St., Camp Wood, 830/597-6195, www.nowandthencottage.com), a woody, country-style hotel. There's also **Mill Wheel** (214 Nueces St., Camp Wood, 830/591-8824, https://millwheelonthenueces.com) on the Nueces River; be sure to call in advance of your arrival. Leakey also has a few quiet cottages, such as **Oak Hill Cabins** (831 Ranch Rd. 337 W., Leakey, 830/232-5555, https://oakhillcabins. com), a cozy wood-paneled haunt with firepits perfect for making s'mores.

Curling and curvaceous, the Twisted Sisters are a west Texas Hill Country landmark that undulate wooded hills and whip the breeze into a Devil's dare. Don't tempt the demons by speeding by. Take these (literally) hundreds of curves with slow appreciation through the Texas sunset. Let the Tejano music on the radio regale you with slow love-sick polkas as you embrace your inner road dog.

Connect with . . .

🔢 Hike through fall colors at Lost Maples

52 Hike through fall colors at Lost Maples

Outdoor Adventures • Hike & Bike • Day Trips • Best in Fall

Why Go: Lost Maples' claim to fame is the fall "festival of colors" when the trees change to beautiful shades of red, gold, and orange.

Where: Lost Maples State Natural Area • 37221 F.M. 187, Vanderpool • 830/966-3413 • https://tpwd.texas.gov

Timing: The park is three hours from Austin and two hours from San Antonio, so start your trip early to return the same day. Visit from October to early December for the most vibrant fall colors. The park is busiest on weekends in the fall, so try to visit on a weekday.

Twelve maples are native to the United States, but only about five are common. Bigtooth maples, also called canyon maples, in Vanderpool's Sabinal River valley are "lost" because they

▲ Lost Maples

have wandered away from their usual areas in cooler northwest states. These rare trees are the color stars of the fall (along with the banana-yellow leaves on black walnut trees, persimmon yellow-orange sycamore foliage, pomegranate-skin red from red oak trees, and muddy apple-red lacey oaks). They thrive in Lost Maples State Natural Area due to the cool temperatures of the limestone rock canyon.

The changing of the leaves has been a major draw ever since before Texas Parks and Wildlife purchased the land, designating the area a park in the 1970s. The park is full of families who make the trek every year, and then there are the new jacks like me who heard local sages whisper about relict maple trees for years before finally visiting.

You can do a day trip to Lost Maples or stay overnight, both of which require reservations made a few months in advance through the Texas State Parks website for people who hope to visit on the weekend. Day passes and camping spots are more readily available for flexible travelers who can visit during the week. Anyone entering the park will need a pass, whether

△ Monkey Rock

△ autumn at Lost Maples

△ fiery leaves at Lost Maples

they plan to hike, bike, or fish. Your best bet is to keep checking the online reservation calendar, which is how I made my first trip.

There are a few ways to get to Lost Maples, but I recommend the route that takes you on Highway 39 southwest from Ingram. In Ingram, swing by Texas' Stonehenge, also called Stonehenge II. Originally built in Hunt, Texas' Stonehenge was almost knocked down before being moved to its current location at the Hill Country Arts Foundation in Ingram, where there are also two Easter Island statues to take photos with. In addition to the photo op, the drive from Ingram to the park is beautiful with no fewer than 10 river crossings and a stretch of road that follows the Guadalupe River for 35 miles.

My own personal sage Addison offered to ride along for an overnight camping trip on a weekday. Between the two of us, we had two sets of carbon fiber trekking poles adjusted precisely to each of our heights (essentially walking sticks), two hydration backpacks with full water bladders (a sack with a hose you use as a straw) and extra water bottles just in case. We also had trail snacks, a satellite phone, and, of course, hiking boots.

On a sunny November day with the temperatures in the 70s, Addison and I checked in at Lost Maples Headquarters, ready to hit the trails. My initiation to the park went well, and I was only slightly self-conscious about overpacking. Plenty of people hike without specialized gear and pounds of snacks. (There's not much reception in the park, but a sat phone was overkill. The trails are well trafficked.) However, I recommend as much water as you can carry.

About 10 miles of trails at Lost Maples include steep climbs that lead to wide views of the Sabinal River Valley. For a cardio workout, try the **East Trail** for a 4.6-mile loop. Along the way, you'll pass by Monkey Rock, a rock formation that looks like a huge monkey head, and mossy green grottos. Steel yourself for two steep, rocky climbs. I took breaks to catch my breath, but families of widely varying ages and sizes all scaled the same paths too. At the scenic overlook, turn around to see how far you've come and take photos of the valley below. For a much longer walk, connect with the other major trail in the park, West Trail, to travel another 6 miles. For something easier, opt for the tiny **Maple Trail.** Really more of a short path than a trail, Maple Trail is lined with bigtooth maples, glossy red oaks, walnuts, and sycamore. It's a chance to get up close and personal with the colors of fall with minimal walking. Wind sweeps the tree leaves down shortly after the colors change, but even as the leaves lie on the floor blanketing the paths in warm rainbows, the effect is stunning.

"Primitive" camping is available, which means hiking in a few miles to camp in an area without running water or bathrooms. There are also plenty of spots to park your RV or car and pitch your family tent near water or electricity hookups. Be sure to read the details of which hookups are available at which spots before you book. Some camping spots also have covered picnic tables and grills. Indoor bathrooms, showers, and a water fountain for filling up canteens are available, too.

Check the Lost Maples fall foliage report online to see which trees have changed color before you go if you'd like to have a preview before you arrive. Before you know it, you'll be the sage leading your friends come fall.

Connect with . . .

51 Drive through the "Swiss Alps of Texas" on the Twisted Sisters

INDEX

PHOTO CREDITS

MAP SYMBOLS

═══════	Highway	①	Thing To Do	⚑	Small Park
═══════	Primary Road	⊛	National Capital	▲	Mountain Peak
─────	Secondary Road	◉	State Capital	✦	Unique Natural Feature
─────	Residential Road	○	City/Town	✦	Unique Hydro Feature
▪ ▪ ▪ ▪ ▪	Unpaved Road	✈	Airport	⟆	Waterfall
═══════	Pedestrian Walkway	✈	Airfield		
----------	Trail				
───────	Paved Trail				
············	Ferry				

CONVERSION TABLES

°C = (°F – 32) / 1.8
°F = (°C x 1.8) + 32
1 inch = 2.54 centimeters (cm)
1 foot = 0.304 meters (m)
1 yard = 0.914 meters
1 mile = 1.6093 kilometers (km)
1 km = 0.6214 miles
1 fathom = 1.8288 m
1 chain = 20.1168 m
1 furlong = 201.168 m
1 acre = 0.4047 hectares
1 sq km = 100 hectares
1 sq mile = 2.59 square km
1 ounce = 28.35 grams
1 pound = 0.4536 kilograms
1 short ton = 0.90718 metric ton
1 short ton = 2,000 pounds
1 long ton = 1.016 metric tons
1 long ton = 2,240 pounds
1 metric ton = 1,000 kilograms
1 quart = 0.94635 liters
1 US gallon = 3.7854 liters
1 Imperial gallon = 4.5459 liters
1 nautical mile = 1.852 km

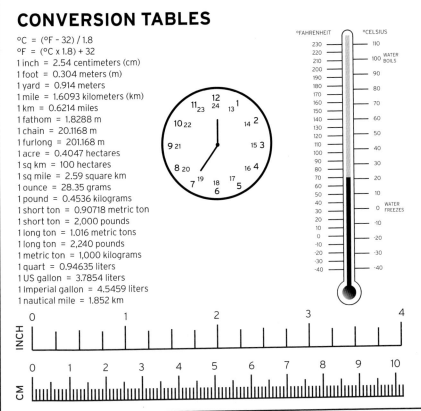

MOON 52 THINGS TO DO IN AUSTIN & SAN ANTONIO

Avalon Travel
Hachette Book Group
1700 Fourth Street
Berkeley, CA 94710, USA
www.moon.com

Editor: Rachael Sablik
Acquiring Editor: Megan Anderluh
Series Manager: Kathryn Ettinger
Copy Editor: Sierra Machado, Jamie Andrade
Graphics Coordinator: Ravina Schneider
Production Coordinator: Ravina Schneider
Cover Design: Kimi Owens
Interior Design: Darren Alessi
Moon Logo: Tim McGrath
Map Editor: Kat Bennett
Cartographer: Karin Dahl

ISBN-13: 9781640495548

Printing History
1st Edition — March 2022
5 4 3 2 1

Front cover photo: © Karsten Winegeart | Unsplash.com
Back cover photos (clockwise from top): © megan markham bucknall | Unsplash.com; Christina Garcia; Bryanroschetzky3 | Dreamstime.com; Christina Garcia; Christina Garcia; El Paraiso

Printed in Malaysia for Imago